Cecil Kirk 1975

**Sermons
for Special
Days**

Sermons for Special Days

W. B. J. Martin

Abingdon Press
Nashville—New York

SERMONS FOR SPECIAL DAYS
Copyright © 1975 by Abingdon Press

All rights in this book are reserved.
No part of the book may be reproduced in any manner whatsoever without written permission of the publishers except brief quotations embodied in critical articles or reviews. For information address Abingdon Press, Nashville, Tennessee.

Library of Congress Cataloging in Publication Data

Martin, William Benjamin James.
  Sermons for special days.

  1. Occasional sermons. 2. Sermons, American.
I. Title.
BV4254.2.M37   252   74-34062

ISBN 0-687-37989-X

Scripture quotations unless otherwise noted are from the Revised Standard Version of the Bible, copyrighted 1946, 1952, and 1971 by the Division of Christian Education, National Council of Churches, and are used by permission.

Lines from "Dirge Without Music" are by Edna St. Vincent Millay. *Collected Poems,* Harper & Row. Copyright 1928, 1955 by Edna St. Vincent Millay and Norma Millay Ellis. By permission of Norma Millay Ellis.

Lines from "The Second Coming" are by William Butler Yeats. Copyright 1924 by Macmillan Publishing Co., Inc., renewed 1952 by Bertha Georgie Yeats. Used by permission of Macmillan Publishing Co., Inc. Published by Macmillan Publishing Co., Inc. and A. P. Watt & Son, Ltd.

Lines from "Do Not Go Gentle into That Good Night," from *The Poems of Dylan Thomas.* Copyright 1952 by Dylan Thomas. Reprinted by permission of New Directions Publishing Corporation. Published by New Directions Publishing Corporation and J. M. Dent & Sons, Ltd.

Lines from "Soliloquy," by Edwin Muir. From *Collected Poems* published by Grove Press.

Lines from "New Year's Eve," by Cecil Day Lewis. Published by Jonathan Cape, Ltd.

MANUFACTURED BY THE PARTHENON PRESS AT NASHVILLE, TENNESSEE, UNITED STATES OF AMERICA

To my wife

Preface

The sermons in this little volume were preached during the ordinary course of my ministry at First Community Church, Dallas, to a congregation of thoughtful people, to whose friendship, eager listening, generous appreciation, and support I owe much of whatever is real in my treatment of great themes.

I am bold enough to think that the book has the merit of bringing together "things long divided"—the main events of the Christian drama and the celebrations inspired by recollection of our national drama and stirred by gratitude for enhancement of life proffered to us by our place in the human family.

While purists for the church year have sometimes treated such mighty events as Easter and Pentecost as theological matters with little relation to daily life, those who treat such national and natural celebrations as Mother's Day and Thanksgiving have often left them dangling without theological means of support, treating them simply as folk festivals. It is this imbalance that I have tried to avoid.

In sending forth this little book I have in mind my fellow preachers, and I offer it to them, not as a definitive treatment of any or all of the themes treated here, but as a series of suggestions as the circle of the combined church and ecclesiastical calendars come around with their inexorable demand—and opportunity—for relevant preaching to people who hunger for a theology related to life and a life undergirded by theology.

Contents

First Sunday of the Year
The New Covenant   **11**

Brotherhood Week
The Shadow of a Great Rock   **18**

First Sunday in Lent
More Haste, Less Speed   **25**

Passion Sunday
Glorying in the Cross   **32**

Palm Sunday
The Entry into Jerusalem   **38**

Easter Day
Rebel Religion   **43**

Pentecost
The Problem of Communication   **51**

Trinity Sunday
Don't Leave Anything Out!   **58**

Teachers' Recognition Day
The Beautiful Gate of the Temple   **65**

Mother's Day
Taking Things for Granted   **71**

Sermons for Special Days

Memorial Day
More Than Conquerors **79**

Father's Day
My Three Fathers **86**

Independence Day
Unfinished Business **93**

Labor Day
The Clay Ground **98**

Dedication of Officers
All Hands on Deck **105**

World Communion
God's Examination Time **112**

Youth Sunday
Jesus and Youth **117**

Thanksgiving
Land of the Pilgrims' Pride **124**

Advent Sunday
Be Prepared **130**

Bible Sunday
Read, Mark, Learn, and Inwardly Digest **137**

Christmas
God Bless You! **145**

End of the Year
Live and Learn **151**

First Sunday of the Year

The New Covenant

And he took a cup, and when he had given thanks he gave it to them saying, "Drink of it, all of you; for this is my blood of the covenant, . . .

Matthew 26:27-28

"Sir," said Doctor Samuel Johnson in his pontifical way, "Hell is paved with good intentions." He spoke with feeling, for his own past was littered with the debris of good resolutions earnestly made and, almost invariably, broken. The premonition that this might come true in our experience makes many of us shy of starting another year by making new year resolutions. But why should we? The Christian life is a matter not of making new resolutions, but of entering into a new covenant. The difference is profound.

When I make a good resolution what usually happens is that I try to summon up and marshall the old resources of my own life, reactivate strengths I once possessed, and make a fresh call upon my will power. That same power which often failed me in the past is revived with a surge of determination, and by the phrase "by God's help," (usually as a pious gesture) to see me through another twelve months. No wonder I, like many others, become tense and irritable. All that gritting of the teeth, setting of the jaw, and clenching of the fists uses up an enormous amount of energy. Yet we often forget that when we enter into a new covenant, there is a new factor in the situation: we draw upon resources other than our own.

I recall the dramatic and forceful way in which this truth was reinforced for me. It was on the occasion of one of my last meetings with Professor Paul Tillich. I was waiting in the lobby of Orchestra Hall in Chicago to escort him back to the campus. He had just delivered a great sermon, and, as usual, people swarmed around afterward to thank him and to comment on his address. They were from every walk of life, from arty, bohemian types in beards and sandals to clean-shaven business men, for Paul had a wonderful facility for addressing his gospel to every aspect of our culture—philosophy, art, psychology, and literature. Some theologians are "religious about religion," but Tillich's concern was with the many-sided life of the modern world and with the light that religion throws upon it. To people who wished to confine religion to religion, he appeared to present something of a threat; they were apt to be suspicious of and even hostile to him. And so it was that evening. There was one young man in the crowd—I judged him to be a theological student from a conservative seminary—who approached him with a belligerent air. Brandishing a Bible under Tillich's nose, he asked accusingly, "Dr. Tillich, do you believe that this book is the word of God?" To my dying day I shall not forget Paul's response. The old man took the Bible from the boy, held it tenderly for a moment, and said, "Yes! If this book grasps you, but not if you grasp this book."

It is not by grasping the book or any other religious instrument—the Sabbath, the sacraments, prayer, or theology—that one enters into the joy and freedom of the gospel; it is by allowing oneself to *be* grasped by the holiness and beauty of God as revealed in Jesus Christ. As a great Christian once said, "To be a saint is not to be good or to do good, it is to be overwhelmed by the goodness of God."

So we begin the new year, not by making new year resolutions, but by entering into the new covenant. A covenant is not something we make; it is prior to all our commitments. It may be that the very concept of "covenant" seems strange to modern ears. We are accustomed to talking about treaties, agreements, pacts, alliances, all things that can be made—and unmade. The field of history is littered with broken treaties, abandoned pacts, discarded agreements. They were contrivances designed to ensure the use of naval bases, buffers of security, channels of trade flow, political tranquility, and so forth. But could one honestly say that we had made a covenant with the people of those foreign states and distant continents? If we could live without them, we would gladly have done so! We are reluctant, or grateful, allies, but it would be an exaggeration to say that we were deeply and indissolubly bound up with them. But the plain fact is that we are. We are bound up in the bundle of life with all the peoples of the world. As Paul said in another connection, "If one member suffers, all suffer together" (I Cor. 12:26). We have learned that the hard way, but we are still far from realizing that the second part of his sentence is also true, "If one member be honored, all members rejoice together."

But it is on the level of our own personal lives that the fact of covenant life is most glaringly obvious, and most tragically ignored. What is a family but a covenant? It certainly is not a social contract. To enter it one has to pay no dues and make no promises. From the moment of birth we are made honorary and honored members of it. From the very beginning we inherit all its privileges; we are the recipients of love, care, and concern beyond all our deserving. "When in the slippery paths of youth our heedless steps we ran," the covenant sustained and supported us. No thinking human being can deny the fact of covenant living when he recalls all the unearned benefits and the unmerited support he has gained by simply being born into a community. That erratic genius Rousseau taught us to parrot the cry, "Man is born free, and everywhere he is in chains."

That isn't my experience, far from it. I was born bound. I was born Welsh and not Scandanavian. I was born male and not female (what a restriction on my liberty). I was born into a certain kind of society, one that believed in education and compelled me to go to school. My forefathers had covenanted together to provide free education for every child and had worked their fingers to the bone to provide it. With the making of that covenant I had nothing to do, but, as I entered into it, what freedom I gained! What liberty I gained as my teachers opened for me the gates of new life, as I passed beyond the irksome disciplines of spelling and grammar, what

> Charm'd magic casements, opening on the foam
> Of perilous seas, in faery lands forlorn.

No one who has attended a great university, richly furnished with books, staffed by knowledgeable professors, and graced by beautiful buildings, can say "Alone I did it." He has stepped into a covenant creation, dreamed, built, and sustained by people who covenanted with God and with one another to provide this setting and opportunity for generations yet to come.

There is nothing mysterious about covenant, except the fact that so many of us ignorantly or perversely elect to live outside of it, becoming more like grains of sand, detached and sterile, rasping and grating against one another, rather than lumps of living soil organically and fruitfully related to one another.

What saves life from becoming a wasteland is, of course, the fact that whatever we do, the covenant of God still abides. "If we are faithless, he remains faithful—for he cannot deny himself" (II Tim. 2:13). Our salvation lies in the fact that in every generation, God's covenant is perpetually renewed by a few people who send down roots and create an oasis because they reactivate the covenant life-style within themselves, and open it up for others.

From among a host of names, I single out the name of Jane Addams of Hull House, Chicago. The inspirational record of her life is a rebuke to pessimism and cynicism. This girl, wealthy, sensitive, and educated, plunged into the jungle of Chicago's ghettos in the 1890s. She saw Skid Row, witnessed hosts of immigrants swarming into the slums around the stockyards, and reached out to them because they were ignorant of the language, apprehensive, exploited, and lonely. Almost single-handedly, she opened the first settlement house in the Midwest. But it was more than a house, it was a bridge—a bridge connecting despair and hope, ignorance and knowledge. When Jane Addams lifted her coffee cup in that house on Halstead Street, she was saying in effect (and I say this in full reverence), "This cup is the new covenant in my blood." There she sat at meals and shared her life. A new relationship sprang into being, the folly of uncovenanted living was revealed, and the reality of God's love was experienced.

I have singled out Jane Addams (although she is only one of many who, thanks to their Christian upbringing and training, have been "grasped" by the covenant) because her example illuminates for me the meaning of Christ's mysterious words at the Last Supper. God is always and ever "he who keepeth covenant and mercy," the Great Father of the human family. But in nearly every human family there are two kinds of children: those who reject and those who accept the love of their parents. For those who allow love to flow freely and let parenthood do its perfect work, their parents become friends and mentors, not nagging custodians and anxiety-ridden censors of morals. So Christ, by his perfect sonship and joyful obedience, reveals to his hesitant children the plenitude of his love. Christ draws us back into the covenant we have foolishly and sinfully ignored and slighted.

As we gather at the Lord's Table on this first Sunday of the new year, let us hear both the promise and the challenge of his words: This cup is the new covenant in my blood. Enriched by the covenant, let us go forth to be covenant-men and covenant-women deeply and full-bloodedly committed one to another, not living in sterile isolation, but, in the words of Karl Barth, taking people more seriously than they take themselves and being with people and for people, but always at their deepest level.

Brotherhood Week

The Shadow of a Great Rock

> *Each will be like a hiding place from the wind, a covert from the tempest, like streams of water in a dry place, like the shade of a great rock in a weary land.*
> Isaiah 32:2

Tomorrow we celebrate the birthday of the man who more than any other American has fulfilled that prophecy. He lived indeed in a time of stormy weather: high winds and gusts of passion. "The rain fell, and the floods came, the winds blew and beat upon that house but it did not fall, because it had been founded on a rock" (Matt. 7:25). That the house did not utterly split in two is due to the spirit and eloquence of Abraham Lincoln.

Speaking to men who had settled into antagonism he said, "We are not enemies, but friends. We must not be enemies. Though passion may have strained, it must not break, our bonds of affection. The mystic chords of memory, stretching from every battlefield and patriot grave to every living heart and hearthstone all over this broad land, will yet swell the chorus of the Union when again touched, as surely they will be, by the better angels of our nature."

Lincoln entered into the presidency at a time of spiritual drought. It was a dry land, indeed, for a civil war is the very worst form of a scorched earth policy. It

Brotherhood Week 19

set family against family, brother against brother, and dried up the springs of natural human sympathy. It made men hard, unyielding, and unfair.

Lincoln's was the only effective voice in that Sahara of hate reminding men of the "better angels of our nature." With almost miraculous calm, he reasoned while others ranted. While others used cheap propaganda, whipping up suspicion and animosity through the devil's art of demagoguery, he pled not for victory but for peace. He disdained the easy luxury of putting all the blame on one side.

"I have no prejudice against the Southern people. They are," he said addressing the North, "just what we would be in their situation. If slavery did not already exist among them, they would not introduce it. If it did now exist among us, we should not instantly give it up." And he went further: "We know that some Southern men do free their slaves and go North to become tip-top abolitionists, while some Northern ones go South and become most cruel slave masters."

That is not the stuff to win votes! It has been said that "politics is the art of confessing other people's sins." In that case, Lincoln was a very poor politician, for he would insist on seeing and proclaiming the faults and failings, the mistakes and sins of both sides. "Both parties read the same Bible and pray to the same God, and each invokes his aid against the other. The prayers of both could not be answered ... the Almighty has His own purposes."

And then he launches into what I consider his finest utterance. "Fondly do we hope—fervently do we pray—that this mighty scourge of war may speedily pass away," seeking to lift both parties onto a higher plane, out of the dry and barren land of partisan emotions. How perfectly Isaiah's words "The shadow of a great rock in a weary land" fits the ministry (we cannot call it anything but that!) of Lincoln.

As the war dragged on, the land was "wearied of its pain—of selfish greed and fruitless gain"—but let us not forget that under the slogans and banners of high-sounding words like "freedom," "states rights," "personal choice," there was a desperate economic struggle being waged. I point it out, historians have pointed it out, but Lincoln never pointed it out. For he was the least cynical of men, anxious to keep the issues on their highest plane.

I think that Isaiah's image of the great rock is very apt in Lincoln's case. I suppose that in this well-irrigated, lush land we can hardly conceive how welcome was the presence of a rock in the desert. Under the pitiless glare and the savage heat of the desert sun, anything that gave shade was a godsend.

But even more: sand was a killer. Driven by the hot winds, it swamped every tender sprout of life, every green shoot with its dead weight. Anything that stopped the drift of sand was a lifesaver. Any large object that halted the drift was welcome. Where there was a massive rock in the path, the shifting sand hurtled against it, swirled around it, and piled up on one side, but on the other side life went on. And if it were not for a few huge boulders, the desert would be endless. The sand would overwhelm everything.

Brotherhood Week 21

In more than a physical sense, Abraham Lincoln was a "rock." And where he stood, he halted the drift. He stood adamant against the way things were going, taking upon himself the scorn, the hate, the misrepresentation, and the gritty lies and the sterile passions that inflamed men hurled against him. When the storm was over, life was greener on his side.

In a word, Lincoln's strength and secret was that he was a reconciler. Where small men sought glory and profit by exacerbating conflict and confusion, where they multiplied (themselves) by dividing, Lincoln had one passion—to save the Union and reconcile brother with brother.

But there is an important point to notice here. What Lincoln strove to reconcile was man with man; not views with views, not opinions with opinions. He was not the great compromiser seeking the least common denominator while balancing one vested interest against another and searching for a formula that would cover everybody and satisfy nobody. He went straight for what is deepest, finest and truest in man, though sometimes deeply buried; he appealed to man's sense of right and wrong, the sense of brotherhood, the sense of moral obligation. With views and opinions he could be forthright, with some views he had no patience whatsoever. He uncompromisingly resisted them. There is scorn (but no personal rancor) in his great speeches, scorn for those who based their ideas on the Declaration of Independence and the Constitution, and then ignored them both.

At Springfield in 1857 he said, "I think the authors

of that notable instrument [the Declaration of Independence] intended to include all men, but they did not intend to declare all men equal in all respects. They did not mean to say we were all equal in color, size, intellect, moral development or social capacity. They defined with tolerable distinctness in what aspects they did consider all men created equal: 'equal in certain inalienable rights, among which are life, liberty and the pursuit of happiness.' This they said, this they meant."

When he saw men chipping away at the Constitution he did not hesitate to expose them. "Our progress in degeneracy appears to me to be pretty rapid. As a nation we began by declaring that 'all men are created equal.' We now practically read it 'all men are created equal except Negroes.' When the Know-Nothings gets control, it will read 'all men are created equal, except Negroes and foreigners and Catholics.' When it comes to this, I shall prefer emigrating to some country where they make no pretense of loving liberty—to Russia, for instance, where despotism can be taken pure, without the base alloy of hypocrisy."

Although Honest Abe was strong in his opposition to views and brooked no compromise with them when they undermined the scriptures of the American people—the Declaration of Independence, the Constitution, and the Bill of Rights—he was ever tender with men, ever concerned to evoke from men their deepest humanity.

So he could say, "Fellow citizens, we cannot escape history.... The fiery trial through which we pass will light us down in honor or dishonor to the last generation. . . . In giving freedom . . . We shall nobly save or meanly lose the last, best hope of earth. Other means may succeed; this could not fail. The way is plain, peaceful, generous, just—a way which if followed the world will forever applaud and God must forever bless."

"Destroy this spirit [of liberty] and you have planted the seeds of despotism at your own doors. . . . trample on the rights of others, . . . and [you] become the fit subjects of the first cunning tyrant who rises among you."

But I would hate to end these thoughts by merely adulating Lincoln. Browning once cried, "Make no more giants Lord, but elevate the race at once!" He knew that it is possible to admire giants and to remain dwarfs.

We venerate great men when we listen to what they have to say to us today. What is Lincoln saying to us today? Let me put it very shortly. I think he is saying:

> In 1776 we conquered our fathers.
>
> In 1862 we conquered our brothers.
>
> In 1975 we must conquer ourselves.

And what a conquest that will be, when like Lincoln, we overcome the rancor and self-indulgence in our own hearts, when like Lincoln we say, in spite of vituperation and provocation, "I have too much respect for my soul to harbor hatred for any man."

We think we are living in stormy days. We forget our history. We forget it was not the flag that was burned a hundred years ago, it was the Constitution, which was publicly set in flames by William Lloyd Garrison who said, "The compact which exists between the North and the South is a covenant with death and an agreement with hell." We too easily forget that the statesmen we revere were lampooned, ridiculed, and called crude and cruel names. Washington, the father of his country, was mocked and vilified as a baboon, a traitor, and his death hailed with relief. Lincoln was called even worse names. But if today tempers have cooled, if the language of the gutter has been modified, we owe it to Lincoln's magnanimous heart and his resolute refusal to make personalities out of issues. Some men are so right that they are wrong! Offensive and self-righteous, they only exasperate and alienate their opponents.

But Abraham Lincoln, in the words of Isaiah, was truly "the shadow of a great rock in a weary land."

> Whom shall I send, and who will go for us?
> Lord, here am I! Send me.

First Sunday in Lent

More Haste, Less Speed

He proceeded to tell a parable, because he was near to Jerusalem, and because they supposed that the kingdom of God was to appear immediately.

Luke 19:11

Today is the first Sunday in Lent, and in a sense we are all "on the way to Jerusalem." From now until Easter it is our privilege to follow in Christ's steps, not only to retrace his physical pilgrimage from Olivet to Calvary, but to experience it as a personal event. But first, let us put that pilgrimage in perspective.

That journey of Christ's is the greatest journey that history records, more fraught with consequences, more important to people than any undertaken by man. "What," you say, "those few miles across the scrub hills of a fifth-rate little country? What about Alexander's epic sweep from Greece to the Indian Ocean? What about Napoleon's snowbound trek to Moscow? Or Mao's leadership of the Long March in China? Or the journey that Lenin made by sealed train to the Finland Station? Or man's flight to the moon? Compared with these, the Carpenter's little stroll towards Jerusalem has been ridiculously over-rated!"

Yet many would assert that in covering his few miles Jesus did more for humanity and revealed more to humanity than any conqueror or rearranger in history. And he did it all at the cost, not of other people's blood, but his own. And when all the boundaries are rearranged and all political systems reorganized, the journey into the human heart still awaits his leadership.

Like Shakespeare, we must ask of the world's Alexanders and Napoleons, "Are all thy conquests, glories, triumphs, spoils, Shrunk to this little measure?" And of what avail is the subjugation of outer space if the inner life of man is still prey to fear, hate, and violence?

Of course, Christ's journey two thousand years ago was short—and slow, miserably slow! That was the complaint at the beginning, from his very own disciples. There they were anxious for results. They thought that the "kingdom of God should appear immediately." And there was Christ, walking along the road as though he had all the time in the world, as indeed he had; but they didn't see it. All they saw and fretted over, was that instead of hurrying for the great showdown in Jerusalem, he dawdled at a wayside well to talk to a faded woman with marital problems; he stopped to chat to a blind beggar; he made a detour to visit Bethany, the home of Martha, Mary, and their sick brother. They didn't see, it never occurred to them, that at each of these stops the kingdom of God did appear, in its power and glory, for someone. They were resentful, restive, and disappointed. And so are many of us.

We're looking for quick results from that kingdom

First Sunday in Lent

of heaven we call marriage or money or a new house or a friendship. We've made quite a journey to get there, and if the results don't show up in the first six months we are aggrieved. No wonder Kafka, that strange genius from Prague, said, "All human error is impatience."

Now, let's look at the parable that Jesus told his impatient followers while they were on the way to Jerusalem. It's Luke who records it, and he calls it the parable of the pounds. It starts out, "A nobleman went into a far country to receive a kingdom and then return. Calling ten of his servants, he gave them ten pounds, and said 'Trade with these till I come.'"

The parable of the pounds is really another version of the parable of the talents, with a slightly different twist and addressed to a different audience. It has the same basic plot, but the parable of the talents had in mind that poor soul, the fellow with an inferiority complex. ("If I can't do everything, I'll do nothing!" "If I can't get the first prize, I won't try at all!") while the parable of the pounds (in which every man gets the same amount) has in mind a more democratic situation, the one guaranteed by the Declaration of Independence you might say, equality of opportunity and all that! Basically the nobleman was saying, "You've each got ten pounds. Don't be in too great a hurry to make a killing with it. I don't expect you to make a fortune while my back is turned, but I do expect you to *occupy* till I come. Dig in there and make the best use you can of what I've given you."

The key word, then, to the impatient is "occupy."

(I'm sorry the modern versions have thrown out that word.) You may be sure I didn't let that word remain uninvestigated. In seminary I spent three years learning Greek, and like the impatient fool I was, I regarded it as a great waste of time (when I might have been doing "useful" things like transactional analysis or office management). But I'm not sorry I spent three years on Greek, just to get the thrill of looking up this text in the Greek testament, to find that "occupy" is *"pragmateuo." Pragmateuo!* Pragmatic! That's what the man said to his servants. "Be pragmatic! Don't waste your time daydreaming and theorizing, get down to cases. Ask 'what works?' Be practical and factual."

But even in English the word occupy is a fascinating word. And it has three layers of meaning. First and foremost, it means to seize, to take possession of, to win. We talk about an army of occupation, soldiers who are there by right of conquest; or we speak of a man's occupation, meaning a craft that he has mastered or a job that he has won the right to hold down. So many people in the world today want to occupy space, especially height: ecstasy and exaltation, by handing over a few bucks for drugs or pills. That is the worst modern form of impatience. They want the experience of the great mystics of the past, but they want to go up on the elevator, not climb the ladder! You get there more quickly by using the elevator instead of the ladder, and the view is the same, but *you* are not the same. "Only the inward journey is real."

The second meaning of the word occupy is to dwell,

to abide. If I occupy a dwelling at 5400 Live Oak, it means that I live there. As my wife will tell you, I don't often live there, but while I'm in residence, I really occupy the place! Home to many people today is simply a dormitory. I once heard a famous, somewhat eccentric, German scholar say that in America, the only place where people really "live" is in the car. They're only thoroughly alive when they're commuting between home and the office. He meant that at the office a man is forced to play a part, like that of the senior executive or the junior clerk. Whichever it is, he is unable to express himself freely, to give vent to his full personality. At home, he is forced to play a number of parts: husband and father, disciplinarian and example. (Don't you think fathers sometimes wish they could just be themselves!) It's not as easy as people think to occupy, to live out one's whole life in the place of one's abode. Many people don't even try. They reserve their best manners and their charm for outsiders. They seem to imagine that home is where you let your hair down.

But let me hasten to the third definition of occupy. To occupy, says my dictionary, is to "fill all the available space." Well, how many of us really fill the space that is allotted to us? Fill the time that is given to us? When some people are with you, you know that they're *all* with you. They give you everything they've got, their whole attention, their entire interest. They are fully present with you. There are other people who can't be bothered. They may have interesting thoughts, but you wouldn't know it because they never express them. You feel they're "not all there." A revealing phrase, for they are slightly mad to act like that. It is silly to waste time making small talk when you can make big talk; it's insane to be in a hurry to talk to somebody else, who is sure to be more interesting, we think, and so never to plumb the depths of the encounters we have.

I am willing to make a wager that there is not a single person who has fully explored the possibilities of anything: a job opportunity, a friendship, a father-son relationship, a dinner party, a marriage, an hour in church. And the reason is always the same: We are more anxious to cover the ground than to colonize it.

When Jesus went to Jerusalem he had Jerusalem as his goal. But unlike some of us, he didn't regard the places on the way as vacant lots. He didn't pass through them in a rush. When Jesus had been to a place, he had been to it, and it was a different place as a result. Something happened there!

Years ago I read a sentence in the book of an Eastern mystic. "Learn," it said, "to turn every incident into an event." An incident is something that happens to you; an event is something that happens within you. There were dozens of incidents in my life last week. How many of them were events? Not too many, I fear, because I didn't stay with any of them long enough to grow; because I didn't go into any of them in sufficient depth. And don't forget: An incident doesn't have to be pleasant and happy to become an event. Some of the most profitable events may begin as unpleasant incidents—a row, a misunderstanding.

But if all we do is avoid it or gloss over it with a sarcastic retort or an uneasy laugh, we may be missing the chance of a lifetime to grow.

This is the season of Lent. Lent means length, long. But it also means slow, as in the musical sign "lento." And my message on this first Sunday could be summed up as: Do not hang back, but go slowly and dig deeply. Take time to savor life, to roll it on the tongue, to get the most out of it. There is an old hymn that bids us to take time to be holy, and we need to learn how to sing it. Why not begin in Lent, by occupying the spaces that are granted to us and by seeking to experience every incident as an event; to turn every "contact" (horrible word!) into an encounter, or better still, a meeting of mind with mind and heart with heart.

Passion Sunday

Glorying in the Cross

But far be it from me to glory except in the cross of our Lord Jesus Christ.
Galatians 6:14

The fifth Sunday in Lent is known as Passion Sunday. It is set aside to give us an opportunity to think quietly about the meaning of the cross before the events of holy week crowd in upon us. And how much was packed into that week: from Palm Sunday to Easter Day!

John Reed, the American boy buried within the shadows of the Kremlin, the only American whose statue graces the pantheon of revolutionary heroes around the tomb of Lenin, called the Marxist-Leninist overthrow of the old regime in Russia "Ten Days That Shook the World." They did indeed, and that is precisely what they did. They shook it. They gave it a horrible jolt. But in the long perspective of history did they do anything more than rearrange the furniture of power?

By the most sober assessment we can make, the eight days from Palm Sunday through Easter not only shook the world, they permanently modified its psychology and they left an indelible impression upon the hearts of men, as the emergence of such martyr-heroes as Pasternak, Solzhenitsyn, and nameless others testify.

The significance of Boris Pasternak, Osip Mandelstam, Alexander Solzhenitsyn, is not their literary genius or their political courage; it is that they have reproduced, in their own careers, the stages of Christ's journey: from the challenge to the citadel of power on Palm Sunday, through the agony of Gethsemane, to the humiliation of Good Friday, and to the Easter glory of the Resurrection, where they come out finally as free men rolling the stone away from the tomb.

Why should we observe Passion Sunday? And why do we call it "Passion" Sunday? The word has become a liability. It has suffered a sea change, unfortunately not into something rich and strange but into something weak and silly. The meaning has become vulgar, cheap, trivial, almost beyond hope of redemption.

It still retains some of its original strength in titles like *The Passion Play* of Oberammergau and in Johann Sebastian Bach's masterpiece, "The Passion According to St. Matthew." However, on the whole, "passion" is now either reserved for the steamier aspects of physical love or blown up to exaggerate a mild enthusiasm, as when people say they have a "passion" for ice cream. But the word, of course, means "to suffer," not to be titillated but to be deeply shaken, to experience some strong, transforming emotion.

I'm beginning to wonder, in this swift-moving world of the twentieth century, where the emotions are battered and bruised by a constant barrage of shocks, whether people haven't lost the capacity to be deeply moved—except possibly by the emotions of hate and fear. This may explain the attraction of such crude exercises in demonry as *The Exorcist*.

The symbols of high religion are no longer strong enough to awaken our response. Even the ultimate symbol of the Cross hardly stirs our deepest feelings. And do you know why I think this is? It's because we are not secure enough within ourselves to allow emotions to touch us—to excite the nerve of pity, compassion, indignation, outgoing love.

I looked up what Kenneth Clark wrote in his great book *Civilization* about the use of the crucifix in Christian art. What it boils down to is this: that it took the church a thousand years before it had enough self-assurance to start singing "In the Cross of Christ I Glory." That's my rough paraphrase, of course. He put it more eloquently and in his own terms as a historian. He writes: "We have grown so used to the idea that the crucifixion is the supreme symbol of Christianity that it is a shock to realize how late its power was recognized. In the first art of Christianity it hardly appears. Early Christian art is concerned with miracles, healings, and hopeful aspects of the Faith like Ascension and Resurrection. It was not until the Tenth Century that the Crucifixion was made into a moving symbol of Christian faith and worship."

He then goes on to say, as though this were a matter entirely unrelated: "It was not until the Tenth Century that the long dominance of the barbarian wan-

Passion Sunday 35

derers was over, and Western Europe was prepared for its first great age of civilization."

Ah, but those two things are not unrelated! They are most intimately bound together, which is why I say that it took the church a thousand years to feel confident enough to sing "In the Cross of Christ I Glory." This makes it all the more remarkable that Paul (facing the imperial splendor of the Roman Empire, the executive director of an organization that had scarcely begun to exist) had such assurance, such confidence in the Man of Calvary, that he should say: "Be it far from me to glory except in the Cross of our Lord Jesus Christ."

Although in most churches the cross is a most conspicuous feature, it is hardly the most conspicuous feature of the preaching that takes place beneath it! That's not because we are not aware of the cross—we are. Perhaps we are too much aware of it, as a symbol of weakness rather than strength. In a theological atmosphere that "glories" in the Cross for the wrong reasons, we talk of "clinging" to the Cross. The Cross is a sword to be brandished, not a post to lean against. In a religious climate where people sing blithely "Christ died for me," "washed in the Blood of the Lamb," and "saved by the blood," I am loath to cheapen its significance.

And what is its significance for Paul? Let me complete the text from which I started out—God forbid that I should glory, save in the Cross of the Lord Jesus Christ, by which I am crucified unto the world, and the world unto me. I can but dimly apprehend this, but I know it certainly means something more morally bracing than the hymns of popular revivalism make it appear.

There are only two hymns about the Cross that I feel comfortable singing, and let me tell you why.

The first is a children's hymn. And you can't fool children. "There Is a Green Hill Far Away" doesn't possess great theological depth, but it doesn't posture and prance either. It is a highly moral hymn—"He died to make us good." "O dearly, dearly has he loved, and I must love him too . . . and try his works to do!"

The other hymn has far greater theological depth, but it is mercifully free of pseudo mysticism and of any suggestion that we can hide behind Christ's skirts to escape the consequences of our own acts, or that the crucified Son will shield us from an angry God. I think the first verse is a stroke of genius:

> In the cross of Christ I glory,
> Towering o'er the wrecks of time.

And that is precisely what it has done. The swastika has collapsed into a thousand pieces, but the Cross still stands.

When Sir John Bowring said, "All the light of sacred story/Gathers round its head sublime," he not only rescued the Cross from the triviality of an ornament, or a magic talisman, he put into eleven words its cosmic meaning. It was not the blood on the Cross, but the Man on the Cross, who provided for him the clue to human history.

> All the light of sacred story
> Gathers round its head sublime!

You may have often sung those words, vaguely uplifted by them, perhaps even puzzled by them, but they mean what they say. It is a play on words, but it is more than mere punning, to say that history is HIS story. If it is not that, it is a meaningless chain of events, "a tale Told by an idiot, full of sound and fury Signifying nothing," or, to put it in less Shakespearean language, "one damn thing after another."

But as Paul, and Bowring following him, so confidently asserted, there is a "light on sacred story," and it falls most luminously from the Cross, for the ascent to Mount Carmel is not one man's journey, it is humanity's journey, "toiling up new Calvaries ever." We are tourists along the trail that he, the pioneer, the explorer, opened up. He not only died for us, he lived for us. In his life and death he is the light upon our path.

Palm Sunday

The Entry into Jerusalem

He sent out two of his disciples, and said to them, "Go into the village opposite you, and immediately as you enter it you will find a colt tied, untie it and bring it. If anyone says to you, 'Why are you doing this?' say, 'The Lord has need of it.'"
Mark 11:1

A church in Minnesota had the bright idea last year of celebrating Palm Sunday with a real live donkey. Actually, the idea came from children in the kindergarten. You know how they love dressing up and playacting. One of the children knew a man who had a donkey, so they borrowed the donkey and got a boy from the junior high to ride it. They formed a procession in the street outside the church, with children of all ages carrying palm branches, lining the road, singing, chanting, and cheering. Although they didn't do it for this reason, they made a public witness that day! Lots of people who never darken the doors of a church, who had never heard a sermon in their lives, saw a sermon in action. They saw the story of Jesus on Palm Sunday, enacted before their eyes.

It was children, of course, who advertised the first Palm Sunday by making the most noise and calling attention to the procession. The bigwigs in Jerusalem

Palm Sunday

preferred to keep it quiet. They hoped that this man Jesus and his few followers would get lost in the crowd and quietly fade away. But somehow the children were attracted, perhaps by the donkey, and started cheering. Perhaps one of them asked a disciple, "What's it all about, mister?" and "mister," perhaps Mr. Matthew or Mr. Peter, said, "This is the Son of David, who comes in the name of the Lord. Hosanna to the Son of David!"

It got so noisy that the Temple policemen asked Jesus to quiet the children. "But when the chief priests and the scribes saw the wonderful things that he did, and the children crying out in the temple, 'Hosanna to the Son of David,' they were indignant; and they said to him, 'Do you hear what these are saying?' And Jesus said to them, 'Yes; have you never read, 'Out of the mouths of babes and sucklings thou has brought perfect praise?'" (Matt. 21:15-16).

Let's imagine someone walking down the street in Minnesota and seeing a donkey. Don't you think he'd be puzzled by it? But there were people in the crowd in Jerusalem who had read their Bibles, who knew only too well why Jesus was riding a donkey and not entering the Holy City on a charger, a fine Arabian steed, or a military mount. He was saying, "Yes, I am your king, according to the dreams of your ancient prophets, like the prophet Zechariah, who wrote, 'Lo, your king comes to you; triumphant and victorious is he, humble and riding on an ass'" (Zech. 9:9). He was saying by this dramatic ride, "Let's have done with conquest, revenge, and armed might. Let's make love reign over us. Let's have done with chariots and horses; let us ride on simple donkeys to show that men have nothing to fear from us."

But you know, and I know, what they did to him. At his trial they brought it out into the open. The crowd shouted, "We will not have this man to reign over us!" The crowd is always afraid of love; it seems so weak. Crowds are impressed by force, by the big battalions, by the leader with a big stick, even if he gives them a few clouts over the head with it and makes them pay for his power in higher taxes!

It takes a lot of courage to believe in love. That's why we have got to hand it to those disciples who followed Jesus on the donkey. I do not think they fully understood what they were doing, but they had gotten a glimpse of the fact that they couldn't go on as they had been. Maybe the world had better try his way of doing things before it destroys itself.

On that Palm Sunday march, don't think the disciples weren't afraid and fearful. In his own way, each was saying what a later poet said:

> If love should count you worthy
> And should deign one day to be your guest,
> Pause ere the guest adored you entertain . . .
> He wakes desires you never may forget
> He shows you stars you never saw before.
> How wise you were to open not, and yet
> How poor if you should turn him from the door.

What a source of strength the children were to the disciples that day. Sure, the children didn't understand what was going on, but to have *somebody* cheering, amid all the scowls and sneers of the cynics, the politicians, and the priests on that march, gave the believers a lift of the heart.

And, believe it or not, we elders feel greatly cheered by the witness of our young people. Even today there are scribes and pharisees telling young people to shut up, bemoaning the fact that youth is going to the dogs. And they can produce hair-raising statistics about drugs and venereal disease. And the figures are frightening—and highly publicized. What is *not* so highly publicized is this event of seven fine, young people confessing Christ as their lord and master. What goes unreported are the thousands of church teen-agers who are involved in civic and voluntary service—our young people who are not merely talking about better race relationships, but working towards it. They may not be shouting "Hosanna to the Son of David" (although they do that on occasion too) but they hearten and encourage us because they are our hope for the future.

But, of course, neither we nor they are perfect, so let me ask how we can join together in that procession behind Jesus. What does it mean to make him king of our lives?

It seems to me that the only man who has succeeded in putting that into verse, is the great seventeenth-century scholar Jeremy Taylor, fellow of All Souls College, Oxford. You might call him the Bob Dylan of his day, except that he landed in prison and Bob has become a millionaire.

Anyway, he asked his fellow Christians to pray on Palm Sunday:

> Draw nigh to your Jerusalem, O Lord
> Your faithful people cry with one accord,
> Ride on in triumph! Lord, behold, we lay
> Our passions, lusts and proud wills in Thy way!
>   Hosanna! welcome to our hearts! for here
>   You have a temple, too, as Zion dear;
>   Yes, dear as Zion and as full of sin:
>   How long shall thieves and robbers enter in?
> Enter and chase them forth and cleanse the floor,
> Overthrow them all, that they may never more
> Profane with traffic vile that holy place,
> Where you have chosen, Lord, to show your face.

The challenge before you young people is not to succumb to the lowest temptation, but to accept the challenge of the highest temptations. For life is full of temptations—to be great and to tread the paths of life with splendor and imagination.

Easter Day

Rebel Religion

Yet a little while, and the world will see me no more, but you will see me; because I live, you will live also.

John 14:19

Today is Easter Day. What does Easter mean to you? In the last ten days I have conducted a little private poll: not a Gallup poll, but a Martin poll. Nothing scientific, just a little casual questioning here and there. The subjects of my investigation didn't even know they were being investigated: that would have put them on their best behavior, and what I was after was not orthodoxy but immediacy.

So out of the blue, I asked Mr. Jones. (That's not his real name.) "Easter? What does it mean to me? What's the first thing I think of? Well this year, being so near April fifteenth, income tax! And hard on the heels of that, automobile insurance. And new clothes for the wife and kids. They talk about 'meeting expenses.' I don't bother to meet my expenses, I just stay where I am, and they catch up with me!"

And how about you, Mr. Brown? "Easter? Well, Springtime—lengthening days, leaves appearing on the trees, Easter bunnies, lilies, Easter eggs, flowers, bulbs, nature rising from sleep, the open air. Everything is fresh and new." Seeing he was getting so poetic, I put in, "As the Bible says, eh? 'For lo, the winter is past and the time of the singing of the birds is come. The voice of the turtle is heard in the land.'" "Something like that," he said, "except that I've never heard the voice of a turtle!"

When I asked Mr. Smith to tell me the first thing that came into his head when he heard the word "Easter," he replied at once: "Churches. I suppose they'll all be full again on Easter Sunday. And music, lots of music. Thank goodness for that, for that cuts down on the preaching!"

And you, Mr. Robinson? "Well, I don't approve of all this commercialism of Easter, all this stuff about new clothes, new hats, the Easter bunny stuff, and spring flowers. I suppose they have spring flowers in China and Japan, but that doesn't make it Easter. I think Easter is meaningless apart from a man who was crucified, put in a tomb, and on the third day was no longer in the tomb. Mind you, I find that hard to believe, but that's the basis of it, isn't it? These soft images of bunnies and lilies are all very fine, but Christianity didn't spring into action at the first sight of a rabbit frisking in a meadow. Sure, there is a kind of resurrection in nature, but that's as old as nature itself. What Easter celebrates, or should celebrate, is something new and unique, incredible even—an empty cross and an open grave. Isn't that what the hymns are all about? That 'because he lives we shall live also'? That there is life after death and he guarantees it?"

Mr. Robinson was the only man I approached in the

Easter Day 45

company of another fellow, and this other fellow broke in, "Ah, come on now, Joe. You know better than that. People don't go around shouting and celebrating because they're going to live forever, but because they're going to live *now*. That's what the New Testament is all about. Something happened at Easter that made life exciting now."

Well, I left them to it while they argued it out, but I couldn't help feeling that Mr. Robinson's friend had the Bible on his side. Didn't Paul say, "Christ was raised that we might walk in newness of life"? Not, fly up into the sky, but walk like new men in a world that had become new?

Christianity founded upon the cross and the tomb is not a design for dying, it is a design for living. What do I mean by this? Many things, but this certainly, if you take the Christian story as a clue, the universe is a vastly more thrilling and mysterious place than mechanists and fatalists make it out to be. It may be *too* thrilling, *too* exciting for some tastes. Remember that jaundiced poet, Swinburne, crying:

> From too much love of living,
> From hope and fear set free,
> We thank with brief thanksgiving
> Whatever gods may be
> That no life lives forever,
> That dead men rise up never;
> That even the weariest river
> Winds somewhere safe to sea.

What a tired, old man he must have been! "From too much love of living." Of course, we needn't take

Swinburne too seriously. For he was not a very consistent thinker. Didn't he say somewhere else in denigration of Christ:

> Thou hast conquered, O pale Galilean; the world
> has grown gray from thy breath;
> We have drunken of things Lethean, and fed on
> the fullness of death.

Why? If he wanted deliverance "from too much of love of living," object to that? The pale Galilean is just his man! He did the very thing Swinburne prayed for.

The fact is that Swinburne wanted it both ways. The fact is that for him, any stick was good enough to beat Christianity with. It aroused too much hope, it aroused no hope. It wasn't lively enough, it was too lively. If Swinburne had kept his eye on history, he'd have had to confess that it was exactly "the love of living" that the coming of Christ aroused, stimulated, and evoked from the men of his time. The "good old days" that he sometimes invoked were not exactly brimming over with *joie de vivre*. Matthew Arnold was nearer to the truth when he wrote, out of a background of classical scholarship,

> On that hard pagan world disgust
> And secret loathing fell.
> Deep weariness and sated lust
> Made human life a hell.

Christ evoked the love of life, of course, in many ways. In different ways for different people. In some he evoked a passion for living, dangerously and creatively, by his example and teaching. In some, he did it by his own aliveness. They marveled that any one could live at such a pitch of intensity while they dragged along on shuffling, aimless feet going nowhere fast!

But above all, he did it because he broke the vicious circle of hopeless fatalism. He revealed the universe to be alive and pregnant with possibilities, not a giant machine, not a passionless, pitiless steamroller moving remorselessly on.

That fine naturalist, trained in the exact sciences but with the eye and pen of a poet, Loren Eiseley, has called one of his great books *The Unexpected Universe*. We are not caught on a treadmill, not shut up in a cage. We dwell in a universe that is open to novelty and creative combinations. That was the disclosure that came to the first Christians and because of it they, too, became bold and creative victors, not victims.

One of the sad things about modern life is the shadow of resignation, a fatalistic acceptance that covers us all like a pall. It is shown in our ready acquiescence in what happens, simply happens, our numb feeling that decisions are beyond our control. It is revealed in the current craze for that new doctrine of predestination, astrology. "The fault, dear Brutus, is not in our stars, But in ourselves, that we are underlings." And like underlings is exactly how the disciples felt on Good Friday. But on Easter Day all was changed, utterly changed. How do you account for it? The teaching of Jesus was the same before and after. The example of Jesus was the same.

As I was pondering this, my mind flashed back to a great little book I once possessed, written by one of the finest Christians I've ever known, the well-loved David Cairns of Edinburgh. It was called *A Faith That Rebels*. That's what was born on Easter Day! The cross was a blind alley. Once again power had steamrollered personality. Harsh realities, the reality of social, political, economic forces had brushed aside the frail tender threads of love and sanity. But most mysteriously, and the records are far from clear, something happened. Something connected with an empty grave, but even more connected with empty hearts that suddenly found themselves bounding with hope.

I call it a faith that rebels. And nobody, I think, has caught the element of rebellion better than Edna St. Vincent Millay:

> I am not resigned to the shutting away of loving
>   hearts in the hard ground.
> So it is, and so it will be, for so it has been, time out
>   of mind:
> Into the darkness they go, the wise and
>   the lovely. Crowned
> With lilies and with laurel they go; but I am
>   not resigned. . . .
> Down, down, down into the darkness of the grave
> Gently they go, the beautiful, the tender, the kind;
> Quietly they go, the intelligent, the witty,
>   the brave.
> I know. But I do not approve. And I am not
>   resigned.

You may say that that's the instinctive cry of a bereft soul. Oh no, it isn't! Instinct has led many to a differ-

Easter Day

ent conclusion: to stoic acceptance, to fatalistic acquiescence. I don't know Edna Millay's religious affiliation or whether she had any religion at all, but her defiant cry, "I am not resigned," could only have come out of a Christian culture, out of a way of feeling, thinking, and hoping that was engendered by Christ and the Christian drama. Read the New Testament again and I think you will have to agree with me that "I know, but I do not approve, and I am not resigned" might well sum up its central message.

That message is not a lawyer's case for the resurrection of one man. Any lawyer who drew up a case and marshalled the evidence as carelessly as the gospellers do would be dismissed on the spot. But, you see, it never occurred to them that in the centuries to come, men would pore over these rapid, radiant documents, plugging every loophole and cross-questioning every detail, as if they were in a court of law. They certainly produced evidence, but it was hard evidence, the kind of evidence that any man could walk up to and say, "What's the matter with you? What's different about you? Why is that gleam in your eye and that spring in your step?" And he would have to reply, "Because I am living a dying and a rising life." Because of that man Christ, I die every day, and I rise everyday. Because he lives I am alive also. Because chance, fate, kings, and desperate men couldn't hold him, they can't hold me either."

That's what I call "rebel religion." A life lived in the confidence that Christ, the representative man, was not history's saddest victim but her most triumphant victor. It is open to every man to live by certain paradigms, certain great personal patterns which history and myth have thrown up for our inspection (Faustian man, Promethean man, men who steal fire from the gods, men who batter and barge their way to success, quiet men like the Buddha who extinguish desire), but for us Christians the pattern man is he who achieved the victory of defeat, who proved that reality is responsive to love, only to love.

Pentecost

The Problem of Communication

*When the day of Pentecost had come ...
they were all filled with the Holy Spirit
and began to speak in other tongues, as
the Spirit gave them utterance.*

Acts 2:1, 4

There are two occasions in biblical history when what we grandiloquently call "the problem of communication" became very acute. Yet on each occasion it was marked by speaking, as men broke out into wild torrents of "tongues." And each time it was like a dam full to overflowing, bursting its banks, pouring forth great tides of water but also carrying with it much debris and engulfing ancient landmarks, and generally, creating more confusion than clarity. This state of affairs usually happens under two conditions—anger and love.

When a man is angry, he may command a perfect pageant of purple prose, but he very rarely makes himself clear. And the angrier he is, the more he shouts, puffs, snorts, and splutters, the less he communicates. His anger is all he communicates, not the reasons for it or the solution to it.

On the other end of the spectrum, communication often breaks down between people who are genuinely, sincerely, overwhelmingly in love, because the emotion is too big for words—they think! John Keats, who was no mean hand at deploying language, has a pathetic passage in one of his marvelous "Letters." Despairing of ever telling his ladylove, Fanny Brawne, how he felt about her, he said, "I want a lovelier word than love, a truer word than true, a sweeter word than sweet." But I will say this for Keats, he did try! Whereas many a less ardent lover is content to say, "Well, you know how it is! You don't need me to tell you!"

The two biblical occasions are, of course, the Old Testament story of the Tower of Babel, and the New Testament record of the Day of Pentecost. One seeks to account for the diversity of language, while the other, registers triumphant victory over it.

I

The story of Babel is, by any standard, one of the great stories of the world. But that is exactly what it is—a story. It is not a scientific exposition of how there came to be so many languages in the world, neither is it a historical account of when and how those multifarious languages developed or from what original tree they grew and which twigs took off in this or that direction. If you want to pursue that line of inquiry, you have recourse to a whole shelf full of fascinating books. For what could be more fascinating than the origin and history of the words we use every day?

I remember, as a red-letter day in my intellectual life (sorry to be so pompous), the very first book I read on this subject. It was called *The Miraculous Birth of Language,* and it knocked me flat! I have never recovered from it. I have never been able to look at the simplest word without some awareness of its pedigree, without sensing the influence of climate, geography, politics on common speech. How marinated English is in salt water! This is the language of "men who go down to the sea and do business in great waters." How permeated French is with the speech of commerce and diplomacy. But while reading that book, it never occurred to me that it in any way contradicted the marvelous story in Genesis, because I had the wit to see that they were not talking about the same thing. One story was trying to answer the question of how while the other was concerned with why.

The Miraculous Birth of Language asked "How are we to account for the proliferating, bewildering range of tongues in which men speak? The Story of Babel is not interested in language as such. It is a bold, imaginative attempt to probe the question 'why?' Why is there so much misunderstanding among the children of men?"

Language, after all, is only one element in that misunderstanding. An important one, maybe, but not all important. That's why, incidentally, I can never get excited about such fabricated, artificial one-world languages as Esperanto. And why my estimation of George Bernard Shaw as a profound thinker went down with a thud when I found he had left the bulk of his considerable fortune to the Society for Simplified Spelling!

If you read the story of Babel again you will see that many languages was not the cause of man's disagreement, though it may have been one of the results. The cause was man's sin, which according to the author of Genesis, took two forms—pride and fear.

For that is the significance of the tower—Come, said those ancient people, let us build a tower whose top shall reach into heaven! Let us make a name for ourselves. Let us (to use H. G. Wells' title) be "men like Gods!" It doesn't take a great deal of shrewdness to see that the desire to be first, number one in everything, is a potent cause of human conflict and quarrelsomeness. I must be the only man in Dallas who has never hired a car because I always forget the name of the firm whose claim is that they are number two. But I must say that if I ever have to hire a car, that is the firm I'm going to patronize. Somebody has got to be number two.

I think that some of the most pathetic people I've ever known were always insisting that they were number one, they had to be leaders or nothing—top dog at home, in the office, even in the church (if they belonged to one although they are usually people who *had* belonged to one).

The other significance of the tower is, that it is a tremendous symbol of pride (monumental arrogance) and a symbol of fear. It has entered the language in the phrase "the ivory tower"—that high eminence shut off from the common herd, sometimes academic, sometimes not so academic. But in the story in Genesis, as in the story of life, one chief motive for

Pentecost 55

building a tower is security. "Come, let us build a tower" they said, "on the plains of Shinar lest we be scattered abroad on the face of the earth." That sounds more like fear than pride to me.

II

I think the Tower of Babel wonderfully illuminates what happened at Pentecost. People, the inheritors and the victims of the Tower of Babel, came together again. Although drawn from many parts of the globe and speaking many different languages, they understood each other perfectly. For they were delivered from the two things that Babel dramatized—pride and fear.

We celebrate the "miracle" of Pentecost, and it was a miracle. Here was a crowd of people from all parts of the known world—Asia, Greece, Africa. The list is long and impressive and is meant to impress us, but don't overlook the fact that they were all Jews or Jewish converts in Jerusalem for the festival. What they discovered that day was not their fantastic linguistic ability, but their common identity which had been growing fainter and fainter after years of exile. And now it all came back with a rush.

Surely the real miracle is that they discovered who they were through their encounter with Jesus, their understanding of Jesus. I think this is a point that has been overlooked and is only in this twentieth century being understood: the more people understand Jesus, the better they understand themselves.

I never believed that I would see the day when Jewish scholars would be writing some of the best books on Jesus, Paul, and the history of early Christianity. But it is true today. Of course, among the broad masses of Jews there is still a deep, instinctive aversion to even mentioning the name of Jesus. As that aversion, that fear, slowly dies out, we shall see it result not only in an improvement in Jewish-Christian relations, but in a deepening understanding of ourselves, both Jews and Christians.

But, let me turn the spotlight of Pentecost on America. We Americans have forgotten more languages than the Jews ever knew. We dumped them in the ocean on the voyage over from Germany, Spain, Italy, Poland, Czechoslovakia, and Hungary—we didn't all come over in the Mayflower. But in spite of our common language, we still have a problem of identity. We are still deeply divided. And that problem will never be solved until we are united in a greater loyalty than patriotism, a more inclusive loyalty than to free enterprise. Namely a loyalty to *man*.

The real miracle at Pentecost was not the speaking in tongues, a rush of words to the mouth. Sometimes I get the impression that in some quarters, speaking in tongues is just another cause of pride. It is a gift in which men boast and glory, an achievement that sets them apart from other people. But that is to erect a new Tower of Babel!

What happened at Pentecost really happened after the tumult and the shouting died. Those divided men discovered they had all things in common, not only material possessions, but their needs, sins, and aspirations. To be filled with the Spirit is not to be simply "full of wind" (although that is precisely the root meaning of spirit), but to be full of the wind of action—a wind that gets behind the sails and pushes forward the boat of life.

One thing that is very clearly brought out in the story of Pentecost—it was a day of power. When the Spirit is absent, power is absent, and then something takes its place which is diametrically opposite. I mean violence. Why is there so much violence in the world? Because there is so little power. Three assassinations and one attempted assassination in the lifetime of even the youngest of us have been committed not by strong men but by weaklings, failures.

Oswald, Ray, Sirhan, and Bemer, all men who resorted to violence because they had no power—no power to hold a job, to create a family, to make friends. They had no inward vitality, no spiritual force. And none of them, you notice, belonged to a church; their most conspicuous failure is that they were "loners." For it is in fellowship that the Spirit is evidenced and experienced.

"On the Day of Pentecost they were all together in one place." One hundred and twenty men who had found fellowship in Christ, and in whom the Spirit found a channel of effectiveness and joy.

Trinity Sunday

Don't Leave Anything Out!

The grace of the Lord Jesus Christ and the love of God and the fellowship of the Holy Spirit, be with you all.
II Corinthians 13:14

There was a preacher in a small industrial town in Massachusetts who preached a sermon on astronomy once a year. He was asked why he did this, seeing that most of his parishioners were mill workers. "It can't have much relevance to them," he was told, "and it has no practical application to their personal problems." "Granted," he said, "but I do it because it greatly enlarges my idea of God."

Now I couldn't preach a sermon on astronomy to save my life, but I am terribly anxious to enlarge my idea of God! because I think that I, as well as many other religious people today, stand under the judgment of J. B. Phillips' book, *Your God Is Too Small!* And I have an awful fear that as the universe expands, or rather our knowledge of it expands as a result of scientific discovery and space flight, some of my fellow religionists are not enlarging their idea of God but contracting it in sheer panic.

There is a wonderful verse in Psalm 147 where the psalmist, without benefit of either telescope or psychotherapy, speaks of God as he who "heals the

Trinity Sunday 59

broken hearted," and "determines the number of the stars." With only half of our knowledge, this psalmist had twice as big an idea of God as some modern Christians who confine God's ministry to the hospital of the human heart and have no interest whatever in his cosmic work. The world to which they confine God is like a big draughty vestry, not the real pulsating world where Christians are actually in a minority, and "spiritual" means not only prayer meetings and dog-eared hymnbooks, but science and technology, and art, music, and painting. Their thought of God is restricted to a small portion of this world and ignores altogether the stellar spheres, the vast ranges of space. How remote they are from Wordsworth, who one hundred years ago celebrated God in the words:

> Thou dost preserve the stars from wrong;
> And the most ancient heavens, through Thee,
>   are fresh and strong.

As far as I can discover, from conversations and reading the church notices in the Saturday paper, few ministers on Trinity Sunday regularly and consistently preach on the Trinity! Briefly, the doctrine of the Trinity is a bold and imaginative attempt to "enlarge our idea of God." That such an attempt needs to be made is, I think, beyond question. And the remarkable thing to me is that the attempt was first made by Christians when the world was a great deal smaller than it is today. Today we live in a bigger world, and we seem to be frightened of it. In retreat from this we seek to reduce, not expand, our idea of God.

In my private preparation for 1976 I have started reading a new and magnificent survey of the spiritual journey of the last two hundred years in these United States. It will probably take me until 1976 to finish this survey since it has 1,158 pages. It is called *A Religious History of the American People,* and it starts in the early 1600s and ends yesterday afternoon—almost.

The author, Sydney Ahlstrom, brings us up to date; he refreshes our memory about the Pilgrims, the Congregationalists, Presbyterians, Episcopalians, Baptists, and Methodists. He breaks new ground for a church historian by taking note of what he calls "Religion in the Age of Aquarius" by describing and classifying sects, organizations, movements lumped together under the heading of "harmonial" religions. Harmonial religions!

I've been waiting for that word for a long time. I knew we had to have it, but I didn't have the wit to invent it. But what a perfect title for those latter-day movements whose chief aim is harmony.

"Harmonial religions," says Ahlstrom, "are those forms of piety and belief in which spiritual composure, physical health, and even economic well-being are understood to flow from a person's rapport with the cosmos."

He is not criticizing any of them; in naming names he is not being judgmental, but simply descriptive. But he does name names, from the oldest of them on this continent—Christian Science, with its various off-shoots, Divine Science, and Religious Science—to

Trinity Sunday

the proliferating variety of New Thought groups, whose best known manifestations are unity and positive thinking. Their grandfather is Ralph Waldo Emerson, and their immediate sire is Ralph Waldo Trine, whose successful book *In Tune With the Infinite* was the first theological best seller to deflect attention from God to man. Or, to put it in my own words, to reduce God to man's helper, his servant, not his master. But, as Ahlstrom rightly says, "harmonial" religion is not confined to the groups he names; it has infiltrated the older denominations, and to such an extent in some that they have lost what used to be characteristic of them—crusading zeal, philanthropic passion, and educational enthusiasm.

Of course, God has the health, happiness, and prosperity of his children in mind, but to use the words of Abraham Lincoln, the best theologian America ever produced—"The Almighty" also "has His own purposes." It is those "purposes" that are apt to get squeezed out when such indubitably desirable things as harmony, serenity, and peace of mind occupy a central place.

I mention these things because it has a very real bearing on the doctrine of the Trinity. In essence what does that doctrine say when you sweep aside all metaphysical jargon? Is it not that "your God is too small!" That if your idea of God is not big enough to include the figure of Jesus Christ, you must break it up, pry it open until it does.

What crimes, monstrosities, immoralities have been committed in the name of religion when men have forgotten and overlooked the fact that God is the Father of Jesus. If they had kept that fact in mind their thought of God would have been not only greatly enlarged, but immeasurably purified. For the Trinitarian faith is this: nothing can be true of God that is not true of Jesus. And how much rotten theology that would immediately exclude! Exclusive sectarianism, bitter wrangling, to say nothing of Holy Crusades relying not on peaceable persuasion, but on the power of the sword.

But to me, the chief boon and blessing of Trinitarian theology is the light it casts on my own divided personality. People make a problem of the Trinity. They forget that the problem is not there: it is in themselves. How does the average man hold together the three (at least three) modes in which he operates? For every man is a son, and many men are fathers. And every man is a weird and puzzling combination of flesh and spirit. If the spirit within him dies, all his relationships give out!

In the long, bedraggled tale of what we have come to call "Watergate," I think the most pathetic and tragic testimony was the unofficial comment—the thoroughly human, thoroughly credible, testimony of young David Eisenhower when asked his opinion of the transcripts. "Well, this is not the man I know around the table at home!"

Of course it isn't! Many of us are one person at home, another at the office, and another at the country club. We don't think any the better of ourselves for that! Many of us are one person with our children,

Trinity Sunday

another with our pastor, and still another with our friends. The problem is to pull these different and often conflicting aspects of ourselves together.

You remember that sad, confessional poem?

> Within my earthly temple there's a crowd;
> There's one of us that's humble, one that's proud, . . .
> From much corroding care I should be free
> If I could once determine which is me.

I fear the poet has got the problem wrong. For the universal problem is not really to determine "which is me?" (Shall I plumb that mystery this side of eternity?) The real problem is "what God do we worship?" One who is divided against himself or one who in himself combines love, grace, and spirit? The majesty of the Creator, the compassion of the Savior, and the inspiration of the Holy Spirit?

In what is probably one of the greatest poems written in our generation, the Irish poet, William Butler Yeats, put off by Irish Catholicism and Irish Protestantism alike, turned to Eastern mysticism, to the occult, and to Irish folklore. But he came back ever and again to the living heart of the Bible. In this poem he meditates and broods over the symbol of "The Second Coming," that doctrine which has been perverted by literal-minded people and is such an embarrassment to many others.

> . . Things fall apart; the center cannot hold;
> Mere anarchy is loosed upon the world,
> The blood-dimmed tide is loosed, and everywhere
> The ceremony of innocence is drowned;

> The best lack all conviction, while the worst
> Are full of passionate intensity.

In our day, the unities of natural life have broken down, fallen apart. Things that belong together have become tragically and destructively separated: rights and duties, love and desire, happiness and achievement, the natural and supernatural, consumption and production. The word religion (*re-ligio,* re-alignment) means to pull life together. It is the sum of those attitudes and practices that enable a man to "see life steadily and to see it whole," to handle it as a unity, and to pull himself together in the process.

Is not this one test of the validity of a religion? Any religion, however hallowed, that separates what God or reality has joined together (flesh and spirit, earth and heaven, theory and practice) and isolates man from man must be suspect when compared with one that teaches and encourages the unity of body and spirit. Any religion that despairs of the world, repudiates it in favor of heaven, and teaches contempt for the body so that its highest ideal of saintliness is a haggard, emaciated man spending life in contemplation of his own navel is questionable compared with one that promotes vigor and health in action.

We are untrue to religion when, instead of seeing it and using it as an interpretation of life, all life, we confine it to one department of life. And so we commit the final Christian heresy. We become religious about religion.

Teachers' Recognition Day

The Beautiful Gate of the Temple

Peter and John were going to the temple at the hour of prayer . . . [and they entered in] at the gate of the temple which is called Beautiful.

Acts 3:2

I am fascinated by that phrase, the gate which is called Beautiful. The beautiful gate of the temple! Like the cities of my youth, London and Edinburgh, Jerusalem was a walled city, and it had other gates, eleven others all together, which were not so beautiful—the Sheep Gate, the Water Gate, the Fish Gate, to name a few. Some of these were just useful gaps in the wall. Through these openings there came the farmers' carts piled high with agricultural produce; the fishermen in from Lake Galilee, smelling to high heaven. The water carriers used Water Gate, for it was near the wells, and through the Sheep Gate shepherds from the hills drove the animals, shortly to be slaughtered on the sacrificial altars.

But the gate called Beautiful stood there, superb and strong—"a thing of beauty is a joy forever." It shone in the sun, bronze flecked with gold; it invited the eye; it beckoned one; it lifted the heart. For it was the only gate of the twelve that gave on to a clear, uninterrupted view of the temple, of its breathtaking dome, its broad courtyard, its noble columns. And, surely, that's where they took the children when they came up for the annual pilgrimage—not through the Fish Gate which led only to the servants' quarters. They didn't want them to have a backstairs view of life, cluttered up with the pigeon coops and the sheep pens, but a view that was immediately glorious and awe inspiring.

It makes a difference, doesn't it, how a child enters upon life and what he sees first? Shall it be a glimpse of splendor or a view of something mean and shabby? Shall it be the sight of the mechanics of living or the sight of that visionary end for which all mechanics exist?

Mechanics are inevitable and necessary, of course. In order for a child to enter into the temple of literature, he has to know something about the dreary business of spelling and grammar. But so many children never get past that. Encumbered with the mechanics, they never reach the day when some inspired teacher opens wide the portals of poetry, and without attempting to explain or analyse, brings into the schoolroom such haunting phrases as:

> There was a time when meadow, grove, and stream,
> The earth, and every common sight,
> To me did seem Appareled in celestial light,
> The glory and the freshness of a dream. . . .
> Whither is fled the visionary gleam?
> Where is it now, the glory and the dream?
> Our birth is but a sleep and a forgetting:

Teacher's Recognition Day

> The soul that rises with us, our life's star,
> Hath had elsewhere its setting,
> And cometh from afar.

What could a boy know about that, who had never seen a grove or dabbled in a stream, who had no idea of Plato's philosophy embedded in that poem? It didn't matter! He knew that he was at the "beautiful gate of the temple"; he knew that life was wonderful and mysterious and that its genesis lay far back beyond his parents' love.

You teachers have tried in your own ways to lead children through the beautiful gate of the temple. You may not have formulated your aims as clearly as you'd wish. You may feel that you have failed to explain certain things. But perhaps what you failed to "explain," you nevertheless conveyed. You gave a child a glimpse of God's wonderful and exciting creation by your own excitement about it. There are occasions when it is better to mystify than to mislead, and it is misleading to suggest that life is clearer than it is. The great philosopher Alfred North Whitehead gave us the wise counsel, "Everything must be made as simple as possible, but not more so."

You stirred in some youthful breast a sleeping hero by your own enthusiasm for the great heroes and pioneers of mankind. You called the roll of humanity's leaders who suffered, struggled and sacrificed themselves, who "scorn[ed] delights and live[d] laborious days," to make others free. They were not always happy men and women, and I hope teachers didn't try to make them happy. You don't have to be happy to be great. And kids know this. I looked around me at a recent performance of *Jesus Christ Superstar* and watched the faces of the youthful audience. They were obviously awed by the magnificence of the tragic hero. They seemed to respond to the triumph of the tragedy more feelingly than the grown-ups. Christ's suffering and defeat *were* his triumph; they saw it shining through. It was not necessary to spell it out.

Perhaps this is where we go wrong in education, especially religious education: we try to spell everything out. Instead of saying boldly with St. Paul, "Behold, I show you a mystery," we surround the shining splendor with our little candles, confusing the children and deflecting their attention from the true light by removing from it all the poetry and romance. It is better to give children something to grow into and to explore than to give them the impression that they know it all.

Worse still (and this, I suspect, is where we fail more than in any other department) we make even religion utilitarian, useful, and wholly moralistic instead of glowing and generous.

I have said it before, the greatest thing a parent, a teacher, can give a child is a high, soaring, view of religion, not simply as a local thing tied to a particular denomination, a particular church, but religion as a passionate concern of the whole human race, as man's attempt to locate himself on the cosmic map. We must show religion as matter that has engaged the best minds of every generation, East and West, from India's Rabindranath Tagore to Europe's Karl Jaspers to America's Paul Tillich and Alfred North Whitehead; the minds of scientists like Max Planck; novelists like Nikos Kazantakis; we must show that religion has given expression not only to theology, but to the poetry of William Blake, the music of Beethoven, the paintings of Rembrandt and van Gogh. Take religion out of life and you strip the great museums of the world of their treasures, you rob music of its inspiration, you gut the great novels of their meaning, you remove the very dynamism of science—all these are religious quests.

But beauty is not only visual and audible and tactile. You lead a child through the beautiful gateway of life by your love and interest, enabling him to celebrate life instead of fearing it.

Sometimes we overdo our talking, thinking we can lecture people into the good life. We need to remember the wise words of a famous educator. "Only the child who is loved is capable of loving others. Only the child who feels secure can welcome others into the group. Only the child who has been affirmed can, will, and wants to affirm others."

I have built this up, and you teachers may not recognize yourselves! You may be more conscious today of the botched lesson, the thing that might have been better said or left unsaid. But let me reassure you! Every time you have appeared in the classroom or hall, you have reaffirmed those children. And can we do anything more valuable, more life-enhancing?

The finest man I ever knew was not an exceptionally clever man, not a famous man, but one in whose presence everyone felt affirmed, everyone came alive, everyone felt that he was taken seriously.

All unconsciously, you have done that for some children, and that might easily be the most important thing you've ever done!

Mother's Day

Taking Things for Granted

Honor your father and your mother, as the LORD your God commanded you.
Deuteronomy 5:16

If you ask me what I consider to be the greatest sin in the world, I would have to answer that it was not pride, not envy, nor any of the things officially listed in such theological catalogs as the seven deadly sins. It is the sin of taking things for granted. And I mean that in two ways: positively and negatively.

Think of the callousness, the coarseness, the insensitiveness that have descended upon us because we take the evil things in life for granted. A thousand years from now men will be astonished that we in the twentieth century accepted such anomalies as poverty in the midst of plenty, such barbarities as germ warfare and total obliteration. They will look back on us as we now look back on the caveman or upon such uncivilized customs as dueling, public executions, chattel slavery, child labor. Little more than a hundred years ago decent men took these for granted as part of the natural order. That's how life was until some intrepid spirit, some crank saw the disgusting horror of it all. Some are awakening today to the absurdity (to put it mildly) of massive unemployment in a land superbly equipped with technology and are crying out for things to be done: homes to be built, roads to be unsnarled, more doctors to be trained, more engineers to tackle the life-and-death problems of pollution.

But there is another and even more serious side to this. More serious because it affects our personal relationships. I mean, the habit we develop of taking for granted the good things of life. It is this that sours friendships, breaks up marriages, and weakens family life. Indeed, I've come to believe that "taking things for granted" is not the eighth deadly sin. It lies at the root of all the other seven.

Pride, for example, is the arrogant assumption that we are self-made men, indebted to no one for anything. We take for granted the unseen hands that hold us, the friendly persuasions, the loves and loyalties, that have given us a footing on this slippery earth. Envy springs from the same root. Envy is the suspicion that we are being taken for granted, that we are not being given our due. Sloth, the drabbest of all the seven deadly sins, is taking for granted and trading on the drive and initiative of other people. Lust is taking it for granted that other people exist for our pleasure. The list goes on, but in no sphere of life does the sin of taking things for granted wreak more havoc than in the sphere of the home. That's why I always look forward to Mother's Day. For if we do nothing else on a day like this, we show some momentary awareness of the most taken-for-granted person we know.

I know some preachers who are uncomfortable

Mother's Day

about Mother's Day. They sneer at its sentimentality and at the rank commercialism associated with it. They see it as a folk festival that, unlike Christmas, Easter, and Pentecost, has nothing to do with religion. It has no "theological content". Yet, what in heaven's name is theology but reflecting on the meaning of human experience? Theology isn't endlessly discussing God, but discussing everything else in the light of God, as he has made himself known in Jesus Christ.

Religion isn't something you impose on life. It is something you recognize as already present in life, already at work in it. The material on which theology works is not ideas and dogmas, it is life itself. And the substance of life is birth, love, and death. It is parenthood and childhood. If religion has nothing to say to us about these things, it has nothing to say about anything!

Do you know why we miss God in life? Not because he isn't there, but because we are not there! It's not because we are so clever that we can do without him, but because we take for granted the mystery and the majesty of our experience. We take for granted the miracle of human speech, linking man to man, the amazing wonder of love's high mutuality, its cleansing grace, its energizing power. It's because we take for granted the truly wondrous institution of the family and its creative custodian, the mother.

When I reflect upon that, I sometimes consider it a blight that we speak only of the fatherhood of God. I don't wish to denigrate fathers, but motherhood is also a clue to the nature of God. And while I'm on the subject, I think it a thousand pities that theologians have nearly all been men. I can think of only a few women theologians on the scene today. If we had more we wouldn't talk such nonsense about sin, for almost inevitably our doctrine of sin is a masculine one: sin as pride, sin as rebellion, sin as thrusting, overpowering aggressiveness. Women have the good sense to know that sin is also passivity, the failure to actualize potentiality.

Years ago I read an article on "The Making of a Mother." Later on I discovered it was a chapter from a book written by Henry Drummond, a Scottish scientist, theologian, and preacher. He wrote his book because he was provoked by Charles Darwin. He did not disagree with Darwin's broad theory of evolution, but because in calling his book, *Descent of Man* he felt Darwin had it topsy-turvy. So Drummond entitled his book, *The Ascent of Man*. And in that ascent he saw the mother as a key figure. I remember the illuminating distinction he made between maternity and motherhood. We take it for granted that they are the same. Not at all, said Drummond. Maternity is as old as nature. Motherhood is as new as humanity. Indeed, motherhood is the point at which humanity begins. Maternity is a biological fact; motherhood is a spiritual fact.

We take it for granted now that mothers care for their children. It was not always so. There was a time in the history of the race when there were no mothers and no children, only offspring, springers-off. The

Mother's Day

children were discarded almost as soon as born, receiving no care and attention, left to fend for themselves. Why, even as late as the third century of our era, a mere seventeen hundred years ago, motherhood was by no means firmly established.

Last Sunday I was reading from one of the apostolic fathers. Writing to Diognetus, who some think was a tutor of Marcus Aurelius, the author made a somewhat flattering comparison between Christians and other men. As casually as if he were stating a fact everybody knew, he wrote, "Christians marry and bear children as others do, but they do not expose their children." Yes, as late as the third century, it was a widespread custom to expose unwanted children to the elements. Children, especially girls, were abandoned and disposed of without ceremony.

We find that incredible nowadays. What we take for granted is not cruelty but kindness, not neglect but nurture. We are shocked when the headlines report child beatings and child abuse. We accept care and love as the norm, forgetting the decisive part that Christianity has played with its insistence on reverence for personality, in bringing about this normalcy.

One of the nicest presents that any mother can receive today is some sign of recognition from her children that she is not only their mother, but a person in her own right, with her own individuality, her own dreams, and her own interests. When we are very young, we are apt to resent this. "I remember quite distinctly," says a great English statesman, "the shock I got as a little boy looking out of the bedroom window, and seeing my mother on the lawn below, chatting with her guests, moving from group to group with great animation and obvious delight. And it struck me like a blow in the face that my mother had a life of her own, a personality quite unrelated to me and mine. It gave me quite a start, and it was years before I got adjusted to it." But that adjustment was healthy, it was a growing point in the boy's life. It was a step forward in his identity crisis when she became more than a backdrop for his own small, private drama and emerged as a person in her own right.

So I would say to mothers: the worst thing you can do for your children is to be everything to them! The best mother a child can have is one who is alive, has interests of her own beyond the confines of the family, has kept herself alive by reading and conversation. The interests can be as varied as singing in the choir, writing poetry, or belonging to the League of Women Voters. Ultimately she must be responsible not to her husband and family, but to God and her own soul.

I haven't been visiting the card shops lately because I'm afraid of running into that Mother's Day card that says things like

> A wonderful mother is . . .
> Someone who gives up her dreams one by one
> So others can reach their bright star . . .

What heresy! "Someone who gives up her dreams one by one" is not a mother, she's a vegetable. A mother without dreams of her own might be a good chauffeur, a shoulder to cry on, a picker-up of discarded clothing, but she will strike no sparks off her children.

It used to be that mother was the conserver and father was the innovator. She kept the peace, and he brought into the cozy, stuffy atmosphere the winds of change, the stir of the outer world. There's this to be said for women's lib: that is no longer true. Today women are the mind expanders, idea mongers. They are recognizing that it is not enough to train a child for the social amenities of life only: manners but inadequate morals, dancing lessons but no Bible lessons, the right dress style but not the right life-style.

When children take their parents for granted, they also tend to neglect their responsibility to "honor thy father and thy mother." Have you ever noticed that this is the only commandment that has a promise attached to it? "That thy days shall be long in the land that the Lord thy God hath given thee."

Where parents are dishonored, where family life breaks down, social, civic, and national life is imperiled. For the family is that small unit in the larger unit where all loyalties are tested, where all the humane virtues are practiced and strengthened. Fall down there, and you fall down everywhere. The family is life's first and most intimate testing ground. It has struck me again with singular force that the men who have insisted most on honoring their parents were statesmen. I pluck them almost at random from the pages of history: the great Semite statesman Moses, the great English statesman, Churchill. Let me throw in for good measure the great American statesman,

Lincoln. And besides desiring with passion the unity of their country, they also had this in common: a checkered home life.

Moses was a foundling with an adopted mother; Churchill had a mother who was incapable of loving her children. There are no more poignant letters in English literature than Churchill's schoolboy letters home, almost beseeching his mother to show some interest in him. And Lincoln's mother was hardly a paragon of the virtues. Yet, it was these statesmen, these reconcilers, these builders of their country, who most earnestly pled for the honoring of that commandment and who honored it themselves. Where the ties were loose, they took the initiative. And because they began there, they carried over into history the same uplifting, reconciling spirit.

Memorial Day

More Than Conquerors

We are more than conquerors, through him that loved us.

Romans 8:37

St. Paul is a surprising man—the boldest, most daring religious thinker the world has ever known. Very few of the normal categories of religion interest him. He rarely classifies men in our customary ways—good and bad, holy and profane, righteous and sinful.

And even when he uses these words he gives them a most unexpected twist. For instance, he talks a lot about righteousness, especially in the epistle to the Romans; but you discover he's not referring to your righteousness or my righteousness. Our righteousness, he says, is filthy rags. The best of it is self-centered, a futile attempt to get right with ourselves. The only thing that counts is the righteousness of God, of which we partake. That's a hard thing for us to swallow, we who mistake Christianity for self-improvement, though great saints have understood it differently; like the one who said, "I pity the man who has not yet found God more interesting than his own soul" or that other who said, "A saint is not a man who is trying to be good or to do good but a man who is overwhelmed by the goodness of God." Or take Paul's use of the word "sin." Certainly he uses that word—but you can't get the Calvinistic definition of sin out of St. Paul. Remember how that goes? "Sin is any want of conformity to or transgression of God's Law." Paul boldly and blithely sweeps all that aside. No, he says, there is only one sin, and we are all and always committing it. Sin is falling short of glory. "We have all sinned by coming short of the glory of God."

Which brings me to my present text—Paul's definition of what it means to be a Christian. "We are," he cries, "more than conquerors." How about that! Is that your idea of what it means to be a Christian? To be a conqueror, yes. To win victories over ourselves, yes. To beat back the world, the flesh, and the devil, yes. How did Tennyson put it?

> Self-reverence, self-knowledge, self-control,
> These three alone lead life to sovereign power.

And many of us are Tennysonians in this, that we value religion and cleave to Christianity because it is the one force that enables us to overcome bad habits, to subdue and subjugate our native violence, and to hold our worser selves in check.

Would we bother with religion if it were not for this? And what is the result? That such religion as we have has more to do with restraint than exuberance, with holding ourselves in than letting ourselves go. And in default of anything better, that's good, I suppose! In this era of licentiousness and permissiveness where

Memorial Day

anything goes, to invoke religion as a restraint and a curb is no bad thing. Indeed, that is how religion has been used over half the world's surface for half of recorded time. What is Buddhism, for example, but a spiritual technique for holding the self in check? It is to conquer desires—those sprawling dangerous desires, from carnal appetite to ambition—that cause so much anguish and foment so much strife. What is Stoicism, the noblest religion of ancient Rome, but another species of self-conquest—the battering down, the overcoming of all that is irrational and sub-human and disorganized.

Now, it is against that background that we have to understand Paul's liberating cry that Christians are more than conquerors. For men caught up in passionate adoration and deep commitment to Christ, life had become more than mere conquest. They were no longer trying to win victories: they were enjoying the victory that Christ had won for them.

And if that sounds a bit pious—more than we modern sophisticates can take—let me put it another way. There are times in every man's life when he has to grapple with and overcome three natural enemies—natural in the sense that they reside within him, not outside of him—the animal, the savage, and the child.

There is a residual animal in us all who longs to reassert himself, who in unguarded moments shows his fangs and licks his chops. There is the still lingering vestige of the savage, the cave man and the cave woman, for whom might is the only right. And within even the oldest of us there are the still-active relics of the child who ever and again longs to return to that world where he was once the sole center of attraction, who sulks and pouts and screams to get his own way. What strenuous discipline we've all had to exercise to "let the ape and tiger die," to restrain the savage, to mature the baby!

And in these triumphs (or partial triumphs, for who of us is yet free) religion, thank God, has had an important part to play. I pity any adolescent who struggles with the dynamics of his awakening body with no assistance from the pull and power of religion. But what is such religion worth if it is only that? What happens when the intensity of desire and temptation has died down, when victory, or partial victory, has been achieved? Has not the intensity of some people's religion diminished simply because the intensity of their problems has also diminished? Where once religion had played a vital part in conquest—self-conquest, self-control and self-mastery—it has now no further role to play. When St. Paul made his famous declaration that he and his fellow Christians were more than conquerors, was he not saying that something had happened to his and their whole orientation, that they had found in the Christian religion a new way of looking at life, that religion had become for them, not a way of subduing the self, but of enlarging it, not a problem solver, but a longing to be used to extend the borders of the kingdom of God.

There is a great difference between a man who is using God and a man who is being used by God, between a man who can only say that he has conquered and a man who can say that he is more than a conqueror: he is the servant of a Great Idea. But notice what Paul goes on to say. We are more than conquerors through him who loved us. It is always love that allows men to be more than conquerors. This means love in the broadest possible sense—not only divine love, but human love; the love of a man and a woman, the love of country, the love of subject, beauty, truth, and goodness. Hate can make man a conqueror, can fill him with furious energy, but only love can make him more than a conqueror, an enjoyer of the victories he has achieved, a creator and innovator.

This leads me to the broader implications of this great text. It is not only in personal life, but in civic and national life that it simply is not enough to be a conqueror. Nations that overcome their enemies have only done just that—overcome their enemies. The broader, bigger thing still waits to be done—to convert enemies into allies, to transform hostility into cooperation.

A disproportionate amount of the world's energy goes into the brutal business of sheer conquest. Millions of dollars and thousands of lives—countless man-hours of planning and scientific ingenuity—are poured into achieving victory. And sometimes in the very process the winners become the losers. In defense of free enterprise, fighting nations are forced to regulate production and subsidize industry, thus becoming nationalized and socialized. In defense of liberty, personal freedoms are curtailed, and the rest of the story is history.

With the wisdom of hindsight we can say now that any nation that merely reacts to other people's policies and has no positive policy of its own may win the battle, but it loses the war. Victory is not a policy. Nearly every victor in World War II came out a loser. A war fought in defense of democracy ended with fewer democratic regimes than when it started: that is a statistical fact.

So Paul was not a starry-eyed idealist when he urged people to be more than conquerors. And that surely means calling upon us to stand up for what we believe, not merely stand against what we do not believe. It means making our own ideals work rather than simply assailing the ideals of others.

Let me try to make this more personal. As I see it, a great deal of personal disharmony and domestic unhappiness springs from our inadequate ideas of what victory means. We often think it means getting our own way, asserting our own superiority, having the last word. If you are strong enough you can do that. But as Clive Bell once said in his magnificent little book *Civilization,* "A man with hooks at the end of his arms may inflict a lot of damage if he brings his enemy down and cracks open his adversaries' skulls, but he can never know the joy of a caress, of a friendly hand clasp." A man with an eloquent tongue may win an argument, but lose a friend.

But what is life about? Is it not friendship in the final analysis? And it takes more than victory to win that. I remember an incident in the life of D. L. Moody which marked a turning point in his youthful growth

Memorial Day

and softened his hard, rebellious adolescent heart. One night, after a stormy clash with his father, the boy was sent up to his room, full of bitterness and anger. He awoke in the middle of the night to discover his father at his bedside asking forgiveness for his rough and hasty words—he was putting no blame on his son but taking it upon himself. That was the beginning of a new and fruitful relationship that lasted through life—and what is more, this incident humanized Moody's religion so that he became the great evangelist he was, an evangelist not of God's conquering wrath, but of his winning love.

What does it mean to be more than a conqueror? Surely, not a weakling—but to have strength enough to ask forgiveness and to share forgiveness; to leap every barrier that separates man from man; to work tirelessly for better communication, for deeper understanding. Paul himself knew this was a mighty task, far beyond his powers. That is why he added "through him that loved us." For it was God's amazing way with him that alone gave him confidence to try it on others.

Father's Day

My Three Fathers

He will turn the hearts of the fathers to their children and the hearts of children to their fathers.

Malachi 4:6

Some years ago I was a fairly frequent preacher at a girls' school outside London. It was a boarding school, and most of the pupils were daughters of ministers. You notice I said "pupils" and not "students." There is a difference; I may be old-fashioned, but I think it is a pity to obliterate the distinction. I wince inwardly when I hear some tiny tot in kindergarten called a "student." Properly speaking, a student is a member of a college; a pupil is a schoolboy or a schoolgirl. A pupil is someone who is under instruction and subject to constant supervision. A student has a minimum of supervision and a maximum of freedom to pursue his own studies, which may account for the fact that there aren't many students! I remember the president of a theological seminary who was asked, "How many students do you have?" His reply was, "About one in ten!"

From time to time at this school, the father of one of

the girls would be asked to preach. And then, this curious circumstance transpired at the Sunday service. If the pupil was eleven years old, she'd be proud as a peacock, as pleased as punch. She'd tell everybody that Daddy was coming on Sunday. If she was thirteen, she'd be a shrinking violet, trying to keep his visit dark. She'd be embarassed, shy, and awkward.

Same girl, same father! But what a difference two years make in the life of a growing child! Between eleven and thirteen a child grows more and faster than she will ever do again in the course of her whole life—and precisely at the time her father, to her eyes at any rate, has ceased growing. Actually he may be growing, too, but while he is growing in appreciation, she is growing in criticism. And rightly so, for she is developing new standards, comparing different models, becoming more aware of herself, and realizing that the hero of her childhood may look very different in other eyes.

Of course, the same thing is true of boys. The so-called "generation gap" between fathers and sons is not necessarily a hostile one; it may be a cooling off period, a season of reappraisement. For his own soul's sake, a young man may have to be a little detached just to get his father in perspective. And happy is the father who realizes this, for if he can bear it and live through it creatively, he will avoid a lot of antagonism and unhappiness later on.

Now I am fond of saying that on Father's Day I really come into my own. I speak with authority because, although I am not a father, I have had three fathers. To be sure, they all bore the same name, Thomas Brinley Martin. They were all the same man—but to me, not by a long shot!

At three different ages in my life, ten, twenty, and thirty, I almost literally had three different fathers. Father didn't change, but I did. And as I changed, I allowed him to be a different person to me. For it is one of the tragedies of being a father that he is not permitted to be the man he would like to be, even to his own son. Because of the son's immaturity he has to hold himself in reserve. Because of his son's needs, he has to play a number of parts which only partially express his true and full personality. He has to be a good example, a disciplinarian, a wise and cautious paymaster, the ever-thoughtful elder statesman with an eye on the future.

However frank and confiding a parent would like to be, there are some things he cannot divulge, not because he wishes to be secretive but because they are things that would load a child with more knowledge than he can handle. The inalienable right of a child is to be a child while he is a child. But I have seen, and you have seen, children grow up in such circumstances, in such crowded homes, among such immature parents who held nothing back, that the kids were little, wizened, old men. They were worldly-wise beyond their age, privy to all the worries—financial and emotional—of their parents, so weighted down with problems that they had no resources to cope with.

I was saved from that, as are most children, thank

Father's Day

God. So at the age of ten I had a father whom I knew only incompletely, and being ten, I inevitably idealized him. Naturally since he was my father, he was the best father in the world. He could beat any man on the block. He was the repository of all wisdom. There was nothing he couldn't do, mend a bike, help with my homework, jump a stream...

But by the time I was twenty, he had begun to reveal gaps that I hadn't suspected. He was not quite the authority that he had once been. I wouldn't go so far as to say with Mark Twain: "When I was twenty, my father was so ignorant I could hardly bear to talk to him," but certainly the communication gap had widened—and that was partly because I was learning more about myself and more about him, and in the arrogance of youth, the comparison wasn't all in his favor! But you remember that Mark Twain went on to modify his statement, and so did I. "When I was twenty my father was so ignorant I could hardly bear to talk to him. But when I became thirty he seemed to have learned a few things, and when I reached forty he had come quite a long way!" That happened to me, too. And it happens to many of us. After we have passed through the strain of adolescence, when we are so busy coping with our own problems, shaping our own identity that we are oblivious to everything else, we get a new perspective and enter into a new relationship with our parents.

My own fellow townsman, the wild Welsh poet, Dylan Thomas, clashed horribly with his schoolmaster father who taught us both English. There was constant antagonism between them. The old man, fiercely puritanical and disciplined, was affronted by the excesses of his son. He stormed against Dylan's life-style and derided his poetry. Yet there is no lovelier poem in the English language than the one that Dylan wrote lamenting his father as he lay dying. All passion spent, the old man slowly sank into gentleness, passivity, and tenderness. Dylan didn't like the change one bit, for he realized now how much his father's fierceness was the other side of his love. So there came forth from the son's choked heart the prayer:

> Do not go gentle into that good night,
> Old age should burn and rave at close of day;
> Rage, rage against the dying of the light. . . .
> And you, my father, there on the sad height,
> Curse, bless, me now with your fierce tears, I pray.
> Do not go gentle into that good night.
> Rage, rage against the dying of the light.

Much less violent, but no less emphatic, is the tribute that John Ruskin paid to his father. As he looked back over their tumultuous years together, he saw what a blessing he had been granted: "In our home, nothing was ever promised that was not given, nothing was ever threatened that was not carried out, nothing was ever said that was not true. Nothing was ever taught that had to be unlearned."

What I'm trying to say is that, to a greater or lesser extent, there is a natural rhythm in the father-child relationship. We might call the three stages of this

Father's Day

journey dependence, independence, and interdependence with the accompanying emotions of admiration, aggravation, and appreciation. Only a very naïve parent would be surprised if they did not manifest themselves in their proper order and at their proper time. But the greatest of these is appreciation, and that is why I welcome such folksy festivals as Father's Day and Mother's Day. It is alleged by some that they have nothing to do with religion. If that is so, I don't know what religion is because I have been reading the wrong Bible. My Bible has a great deal to say about fathers, mothers, and children. Such theology as it contains is inextricably bound up with personal relationships—and what personal relationships are more crucial and more vital than those at the heart of the family? This is the very stuff of life in which God reveals himself.

Does it not seem remarkable to you that for over twenty centuries, the highest title we have been able to find for God is father? Not king, judge, lord, or master, but father in spite of all our unsatisfactory relationships and our temporary disenchantments with our own fathers.

Which came first, the chicken or the egg? God's Fatherhood leading us to believe in an ideal fatherhood here on earth? Or some experience of human fatherhood lighting up the character of the Divine Mind? In these matters there is no first or last since both belong together. Which is why, perhaps, the best symbol of religious life is the vision granted to Jacob at Peniel, when he saw the ladder set up between heaven and earth and the angels of God ascending and descending upon it. Life is a two-way street. What we know of God makes us aware of each other. What we know of each other makes us knowledgeable about God.

Independence Day

Unfinished Business

Have you not read what David did?
Matthew 12:3

The Feast of Passover, of which the Communion Service is a fulfillment and an extension, marked for the Children of Israel a new birth of freedom. "We were Pharaoh's bondmen in Egypt, and the Lord brought us out by a mighty hand." It marks the stage at which a rabble of Semitic tribes became one people, "one nation under God," when they threw off the yoke of slavery and embarked on the perilous pilgrimage of freedom.

The Fourth of July, the glorious fourth, is also a festival of freedom, a celebration of national identity. I think we are inclined to overlook that these days. The Fourth has become a generalized patriotic event. Indeed, after taking a private poll, I discover that to many people it has no specific content other than an opportunity to demonstrate that they are good Americans, proud of their country, proud of their flag. But if we are to celebrate it in a valid way we have to attach it to a very specific, historical occasion. We must remember a decision painfully, reluctantly, and agonizingly arrived at—to break loose from paternalism, to come of age. Not everything about British rule was tyrannical: taxation, yes, but there was also protection, the shield of a great navy and a trained army in case of foreign invasion. Yet in spite of this, the urge for freedom, even if it put the young nation in peril, was too strong to resist.

The Fourth of July was a venture of faith, not a mere gesture of rebellion. And it raised as its standard, not a flag but a document—the Declaration of Independence. That document, of course, is rooted in the Scriptures. Not only are its phrases lifted from the Bible in general terms, but they are definitely linked with the experience of the chosen people. They echo and reflect the Passover syndrome: slavery in Egypt, the flight into the wilderness, the great trek to the promised land, and over all, the guiding hand of God.

Now, I would link these two events together by recalling a question that Jesus put to his countrymen two thousand years ago. The question is this: "Have you never read what David did?" I think Jesus raised that question on the equivalent of our Fourth of July! Looking around at his countrymen, self-satisfied and set in their ways, he recalled one of their great national heroes. "Have you never read what David did?" on that memorable day when the savior of his people stumbled into the house of God seeking refuge from his enemies? He was on the run, desperate with fatigue and hunger. Inside the sanctuary, to the horror of the priest, he lurched up to the altar and seized the shewbread displayed on the holy table. He took the

Independence Day 95

consecrated bread and tore into it with ravenous teeth! That's what David did. Remember?

Then, fortified in body, he cast around for some means of renewing the fight with his enemies. "Are there no weapons of war here?" he asked, "for I have fled in haste and brought nothing with me." To which the dazed custodian replied, "The sword of Goliath whom you slew in the Valley of Elah, behold that is here, wrapped in a cloth behind the ephod. There is none other save that here." David lifted up his head. The sword of Goliath! Of course, that's where it was. Safely stowed away as a trophy. It all came back to him now. When he had defeated the Philistine on that memorable day, the crowd had surged forward and carried off his "terrible swift sword" to God's house as exhibit A. David had almost forgotten its existence. But now he was back on the plains of Elah, the shepherd boy, ruddy and slim and strong, with pounding heart and dry mouth facing the giant. And with no more ado, he cried out, "There is none like that! Give it to me!" And the sword flashed into action again.

"Have you never read what David did?" asked Jesus. Of course they had. But that was history, safely embalmed in the dim and hallowed past. Like the Declaration of Independence to many of us, not a document for daily use but a revered showpiece, a precious relic.

There is an obvious and painful parallel here with what happens to Christianity. It so happens that I have been reading the *Life of Erasmus*. (Erasmus, thou shouldst be living at this hour!) Because he was the mediator among the reformers, he didn't make much impact on the Germans (Luther and his extremism were more to their taste), but he had a great influence on English theology and on English personalities. One of the Englishmen whom Erasmus profoundly influenced was Linacre, physician to King Henry the Eighth and founder of the Royal College of Surgeons. His influence was so great that Linacre gave up the practice of medicine and entered the church. It was then, believe it or not, that he read the New Testament for the first time. He is reported to have said, "Either this isn't the Gospel, or we are not Christians!" Something like that happens when some people read the Declaration of Independence for the first time— "Either this isn't Americanism, or we are not Americans!"

To the early Christians the fellowship meal was not a picnic, it was a declaration of independence. They gathered in Christ's name to pluck up courage to live as Christians in a hostile world. It was not the bread that fortified them, but what the bread stood for: sharing, dependence, and loyalty one to another, bread as it passed from hand to hand with the blessing of Christ on it. When we take this bread, we declare our independence here from every form of clinging subservience to the world, the flesh, and the devil. We break free from Egypt, from every form of tyranny to journey to our promised land. We celebrate, not something accomplished, but a promise still to be implemented. Gabriel Marcel, the French playwright-philosopher, when converted to Christianity, wrote: "I can in no sense boast of having arrived. All I can say is that some parts of me have struggled up into the light, but much remains in the dark, much of me remains waiting to be evangelized."

As we read the story of what David did with the sword that he had wrested from the hand of Goliath and then forgotten, remember—Nothing we give to God is ever lost! In the great hours of crisis it is there, to be drawn upon again. What we have stored up in good times—discipline, prayer, worship—is there waiting to be used. No life suddenly collapses. There is always a history of defeat, defeat in small secret ways, a hidden accumulation of carelessness, slackness, self-indulgence. Only he who has won something can say in the hour of testing, "There is none like that! Give it to me!"

Labor Day

The Clay Ground

All these vessels in the house of the Lord . . . were of burnished bronze. In the plain of the Jordan the King cast them, in the clay ground between Succoth and Zarthan.
I Kings 7:45-46

One of the advantages of daily Bible reading, hard going as it sometimes is when one has to plough through lists of names and places, is that one always comes up with a nugget of pure gold in the midst of all the slag. This happened to me last week. Thinking about the homiletical problems presented by Labor Day, I stumbled across this sentence in the history of King Solomon: The vessels of the king's house, which were of bright bronze, were cast in the clay ground between Succoth and Zarthan.

There's an awful lot of clay ground in life. In everybody's life! For Solomon it lay between Succoth and Zarthan. I didn't bother to look that up on the map because I know it well. It's that heavy stretch between making a living and making a life. It's that dreary patch that lies between where we are and where we want to go. For some people it lies between home and work—that unproductive area they simply have to traverse in order to get to somewhere else! For far too many people in our society it lies within the work

Labor Day

itself, perhaps in a job that yields no delight—hard clay-like stuff from which they get no pleasure or inward profit.

At a dinner party the other night, partly to make conversation but also because I was genuinely interested, I asked the host—an attorney in his early forties—what he was doing now. As if he had been waiting all day to tell me, he said, "Doing? Nothing; I'm just drifting. I'm stuck!" And I daresay there come moments in every man's life when he feels that way; either because he has mastered the job which has now become a matter of routine or because he suddenly discovers he's in the wrong job, yet lacks the courage or the opportunity to get out of it.

But let me hasten to add: this isn't a question of age. People get stuck at forty, but they get stuck at fourteen too! In fact, I sometimes think that adolescence is the supremely "sticky" period of life. I know it was for me, and I don't think I was an exception.

I go back again and again to those marvelous words of John Keats. I don't know anyone who has described more poignantly what it means to be an adolescent. "The imagination of a boy is healthy, and the mature imagination of a man is healthy; but there is a space of life between, in which the soul is in a ferment, the character undecided, the way of life uncertain, the ambition thick-sighted: thence proceeds mawkishness, and the thousand bitters." There's clay ground for you—heavy, intractable stuff that many a sensitive youngster encounters in the teen years.

We talk about the wisdom of Solomon. He was

never wiser than in his handling of that bit of wasteland between Succoth and Zarthan.

It was an eyesore, and many a lesser man would have let it prey on his mind. You know how it is. The ugly things of life loom so large that they blot out everything else. Somewhere in Emerson there is a little poem—

> He who has a thousand friends has not a friend to spare,
> And he who has one enemy shall meet him everywhere.

Give us one unpleasant fact, and it covers the whole landscape; it looms so large that we have eyes for nothing else. So it was, at first, with Solomon. Everywhere he looked the smiling fields, the lush meadows, the rich vineyards were blotted out; he saw nothing but that drab eyesore. It was becoming an obsession with him until he realized that to get rid of an obsession one had to make a concession. He gave up his attempt to make it a beautiful place: instead he concentrated on making it useful. He discovered that, while nothing would grow in it, it was an ideal place for casting brass. And it was there, in the clay ground between Succoth and Zarthan, that eventually all the bronze ornaments of the royal household were produced.

This is a parable about life. What do you do about the clay ground of life? We all have it, some greater, some less. I know a man for whom the heavy soil of his existence was the job he felt he'd been stuck with. When I first knew him, although still a young man, he was on the way to becoming frustrated and embittered. And then one day, although these things are never sudden, he realized that there was only one course left open to him. Since he couldn't change his job, he'd better set about changing his attitude to it. He began to search for those opportunities within the work itself which he'd been ignoring, those openings and advantages that, up to now, he had despised. I won't conceal from you the fact that I'm talking about a minister—and what a lot of frustrated ministers there are!

He told me that one factor in his conversion—and it was nothing less—was a remark I once quoted in a lecture. I've even forgotten who said it. It was, I think, a Scottish preacher ministering to a tiny congregation in a remote village. "One soul is a big enough parish for any man!" he said when people commiserated with him on his sparse flock.

I want to return to the clay ground of adolescence. In this connection I must say that if adolescents were left to themselves, they might wriggle out of it far better than they do! It seems to be to somebody's interest, usually a financial interest, to keep them wallowing in the mire of self-pity and confusion!

Andrew Fletcher said, "If a man were permitted to make all the ballads, he need not care who should make the laws of the nation." Have you listened to those songs lately—the words I mean? Many of them scorn working for a living. They pity the poor souls who drudge away "from nine to five, just to prove that they're alive."

Now you may be sure of one thing—it didn't take

him from nine to five to write that! But think of the mood it expresses! Sure, it sees one thing clearly enough—that work, whether nine to five or 8:30 till 6:30 is precisely what does keep many people alive. It gives them whatever dignity and identity they possess. But what's wrong with that?

What seems to a restless teen-ager like routine is frequently the cause of inward excitement, of firm identity, of dramatic inner development for some people. Just as to emerge victor in a moral struggle is the greatest triumph a man can experience, so there is a moral quality also, a deep abiding satisfaction, in taking the clay ground of making a living and casting in unpromising soil the bright ornaments of greater productivity, of more jobs, of a dynamic economy with expanding opportunities for all.

But the clay patches of life are not all outside of us. There are hard, barren patches within also. In every personality, there is something obdurate and stiff, unyielding and unattractive. It may be a matter of temperament—in some a weakness of the body, in others a strain of melancholy, a certain woodenness of mobility. The abrupt division of people into saints and sinners, good and bad, has always seemed to me to be unreal. It ignores the fact that some people are endowed with lightness of touch, some are heavy-handed; there are people whose bodies help them to express the thoughts that are in them, while others have a physical make-up that never becomes plastic to their inner spirit; there are people whose goods are all in the shop window, immediately available to all, while others instinctively keep their best goods in the vault behind.

The problem is how to make the best of all this. Booker T. Washington once said, "Character is the sum of all we have struggled against."

Did you ever read Emerson's essay "Compensation?" There is some compensation in every defect. It has often been remarked that tall people are inclined to take things within their stride; they are naturally inclined to look down from a superior height. It's the little men who have to strive. But they may strive either to put themselves on the map—in which case they become aggressive and touchy—or they may turn their physical inadequacy to constructive use. But this is really a trifle. The biggest handicaps people suffer are more deep-seated than that—a congenital inferiority, an inborn tendency to depression, a low degree of vitality, a natural timidity, an almost crippling shyness.

But all is not lost if a man will work this clay ground in the right way. I doubt whether in the history of mankind there has been a more clay-like man than St. Paul. He was ugly, short, with a thorn in the flesh (possibly epilepsy), but he was a man who discovered that "When I am weak, then I am strong." For his weakness and physical handicap made it impossible for him to trade on easy animal charm, made it imperative that he dig down to find deeper sources of power in God.

One of my favorite poets is the Irish writer, William

Butler Yeats. Somewhere he makes the remark, "Out of our quarrel with others we make rhetoric." That's a very Irish remark. Everybody knows how eloquent Irishmen are when they're fighting mad. But, says Yeats, "Out of our quarrel with ourselves we make poetry." Rhetoric is what inflames; poetry is what reveals.

If all of us, young and old alike, spent as much time quarreling with ourselves as we do with circumstances, conditions, outward events—what a transformation there might be! There is a line in Jeremiah that suggests an even deeper and more productive quarrel. "The Lord has a controversy with his people," says the prophet. Out of that controversy there can come, if we let it, from the most clay-like ground, vessels of shining splendor.

Dedication of Officers

All Hands on Deck

Would that all the Lord's people were prophets, that the Lord would put his spirit upon them!

Numbers 11:29

That inimitable humorist, God's gift to America, Will Rogers once remarked that he was not a member of any organized political party—he was a Democrat! That wisecrack is as fresh today as it was way back in the 1930s. And *mutatis mutandis*, it is equally applicable to the other party.

What the patron saint of Oklahoma said about a political party applies with equal force to democracy as such. It is always in a state of disarray—disorganized and dissenting. And long may it continue to be so!! Some people deplore this, but not I. I agree with Winston Churchill, who said that democracy is the most inefficient, cumbersome, creaking form of government ever devised, and the best!

I would rather belong to a nation of dissenters, learning how to dissent creatively and to reach a slow consensus, than belong to a mob of yes-men shouting "Heil Hitler." A man loses his self-determination, self-responsibility, and self-initiative when he ceases to think for himself. But then, I am in a modest and inadequate way, a Christian and a churchman. A healthy church is not one in which all dissent is flattened out, but one in which there is freedom to speak out and to be spoken to.

If I seem to drag in the church here, it is because the relationship between church and democracy is a very close one indeed. Without minimizing the enormous contribution made to the idea and practice of democracy by the ancient Greeks, I think the full surge of the democratic idea owes its impetus to the Hebrews. Particularly through Moses who cried so long ago, "Would that all the Lord's people were prophets, that the Lord would put his spirit upon them!" It is that cry, echoing and reechoing through two centuries that has given birth to many of the things we cherish in this broad land: respect for the individual, desire for his participation in his own progress and destiny, emphasis on universal education, and confidence in the jury system.

Of course, with the wisdom of hindsight, it might appear to us now that Moses was simply being sensible in publicly and officially sharing the burden of leadership with others. But in that day and place such concepts as delegating responsibility and decentralizing authority were unthought of and utterly without precedent. Even more without precedent was his next step. As we heard it read, there arose an occasion

Dedication of Officers

when two young men, Eldad and Medad, dared to exercise the functions of spiritual leadership. Since they were unauthorized persons, laymen without benefit of ordination, this immediately provoked a wave of protest culminating in Joshua's going to his commander-in-chief and saying, "My lord Moses, forbid them!" It was then that the spirit of Moses was displayed in all its magnanimous breadth and depth. "What!" he cried. "Are you jealous for my sake? Would that all the Lord's people were prophets, that the Lord would put his spirit upon them!" For my money, that is the real charter of democracy. Democracy is not some lever-pulling arrangement that gives "one man, one vote." It is a passionate desire to involve the maximum number of people in the maximum number of decisions at their maximum depth. In this way people are not only helped, but they help themselves to grow.

Now there is, as I have suggested, a direct line between the democratic ideal and religion. Lincoln's hallowed words about democracy being a "government of the people, by the people, for the people" were not the rhetorical invention of some prairie lawyer. He lifted those words bodily from John Wycliffe's translation of the Bible. In 1382, when Wycliffe finished his massive task of "englishing" the Bible so that, as he put it, "the plowman in the field and the weaver at the loom might hear the Word of God in his own tongue," he wrote a preface which said, "The Bible is for the government of the people, for the people, by the people." Government solely of the people is tyranny;

government for the people is paternalism, which is a subtle form of tyranny; only *of, for,* and *by* the people is it government that produces men not boys, free men, not slaves.

What has all this to do with the dedication of officers? This: we are not doing something that concerns us alone. This dedication is not some private ritual of a religious club; we are strengthening and reaffirming the very basis of our democratic way of life. As long as there are enclaves of people accepting responsibility and demonstrating leadership within the organizations to which they belong, the body politic is healthy. And this is true of all organizations, from PTAs to Trade Unions. During the depression I saw a very powerful union, the Electrical Workers Union, fall into the hands of communist leadership mainly because there was no other leadership available. The great mass of the membership paid their dues and then sat back, leaving such boring jobs as committees to a few fanatics. About that time James Agate said, three things will save England from revolution: the pubs, the pictures, and the pools. All the time a silent revolution was going on and might have succeeded, had not the tricks and machinations of a tiny minority become too blatant, forcing the moderate membership to rise in wrath and throw them out.

I am sometimes irritated by those people who believe in religion, but not in institutional religion. Some people think it is good for a community to be honeycombed with churches and other redemptive agencies, but do nothing either to support them or make

Dedication of Officers

them grow. These may be the same people who decry the moral permissiveness of our time, deplore youth's absence of moral standards and moral stamina, and yet do not lift a finger to maintain, much less actively support, the efforts of those who work at promoting them.

It may be that that word "prophet" has a scary sound to your ears. It is at least three sizes too big to cover anything you envisage yourself doing. It has a warning and a scolding tone that jars your easygoing temperament. But don't forget the chief function of a prophet is not to predict but to reveal; it is not to shout and holler but to interpret. And we can all do that, whether we intend to or not. Perhaps we do it most effectively when we don't intend to do it. By the way we handle our own lives, we show that we believe life is worth living and worth living well and that we are not irresponsible mavericks, but people who hold ourselves responsible to God and are motivated by his son Jesus Christ.

But in dedicating these appointed officers, I am looking beyond them to the general membership, whom they represent. We are all in this together. When Luther promulgated the hallowed Protestant doctrine of the priesthood of all believers, when he put into German what Moses had said in Hebrew, he was not seeking to minimize the priesthood but to increase it, to broaden its scope, not to downgrade the church official, but to upgrade the common life. I would, he said, that every man were a priest to his brother, that the father were a priest to his son, the husband to his wife, the teacher to his student, the employer to his staff, the doctor to his patient, the lawyer to his client. It was not merely the professionalism of the clergy that he was attacking, but the professionalism of all who limit their tasks to what must be done and can be done without involving themselves in other people's lives.

How badly we need the Mosaic and Lutheran call to human priesthood today! Never more so, for our society is honeycombed with little centers of selfishness. The very idea of priestly concern, of mediating God and goodness, of accepting responsibility and of caring has given place to rampant self-regard and self-expression, so that almost at the drop of a hat you find partner deserting partner when his little ego is thwarted, when personal happiness is not instantly and painlessly forthcoming.

"Would that all the Lord's people were prophets"—priests and pastors! Seeking and finding life, not in self-expression but in self-realization, which is a very different thing. For how can we properly realize ourselves if we live in isolated selfishness? How can we grow except by helping others to grow and growing along with them. We must rejoice in their growth and benefit from it.

We have almost forgotten what it means to think like that. Alas, nearly all the pressures of modern life from the printed page, the silver screen, the air waves, to popular psychology seem to stress the right of the naked individual to be happy. As if such a thing could ever be! As if man could ever be a person (a religious category) without being intertwined with others, finding life as he loses it, saving life as he shares it. Across the centuries we hear the pleading prayer, "Would that all the Lord's people were prophets!" and say, "Here am I, Lord, send me!"

World Communion

God's Examination Time

Let a man examine himself...
I Corinthians 11:28

Examine yourselves, to see whether...
II Corinthians 13:5

Somebody once made the suggestion that every college graduate should be shipped back to school at the end of every five years to see if he still deserved his B.A. degree. I think I can guess where that suggestion came from. Certainly not from the graduates, for who of us would survive that test? I think it came from some disenchanted employer, maybe a publisher or head of a law firm who had hired a bright young man, with impeccable paper credentials who turned out to be a disappointment. He had his sheepskin to prove he had passed his examinations, but he had ceased to examine himself. And now, with the pressure off his back, he was not climbing but coasting. Some statistics I saw lately on reading after college would seem to bear this out. They showed that a shocking percentage of graduates hadn't opened a book in months; some had put books aside altogether.

Now, something like this must have been in Paul's mind when he wrote to the Christian graduates in Corinth. Not once, but twice he uses the word "examine" as if he were aware that even in those very early days of the church, some people had stopped growing, stopped learning and were due for a checkup. And since the first occasion on which he used this word "examine" was at the communion service, it seems appropriate that we should begin there.

I can remember my first communion and the sobering effect it had on me as though it were yesterday. My patriarchal minister read out in his solemn voice: "Whosoever shall eat this bread and drink this cup of the Lord unworthily, shall be guilty of the body and blood of the Lord. But let a man examine himself and so let him eat of that bread and drink of that cup, for he that eateth and drinketh unworthily, eateth and drinketh damnation to himself, not discerning the Lord's body." It sent a shiver down my spine, and I wondered how anybody, myself included, could dare to approach the table with those words resounding in their ears. Later on when I went to Scotland I discovered that many people, particularly in the remote Highlands among the crofters and fisherfolk where they take their religion with awesome seriousness, had attended church every Sunday of their lives but had never dared to go forward to the Communion Table. They hung back. They did not feel that they were worthy. I felt then, young as I was, that they were wrong but I didn't know why. I see it now.

If "unworthy" meant morally imperfect, they were right to stay in their pews, but in that sense are we not all unworthy? If "unworthy" meant sinful, are we not all unworthy? As Paul himself said in another connection, "All have sinned and come short of the glory of God," and in another place even more emphatically, "There is none righteous, no not one!" And then it struck me. Of course, the unworthiness has nothing to do with achievement, with failure or success. It is a matter of attitude. What is your attitude as you come to the Lord's table? It is worthy if you "discern the Lord's body." It is unworthy if you do not discern the Lord's body.

But that presents difficulties of its own. That seems to require of us a kind of mystical fervor, a kind of spiritual second sight which few of us possess by which we *see* Christ's actual body in the bread. But that isn't the meaning at all, despite some theologies. For remember this: when Paul speaks of the body of Christ, he invariably, and consistently means the "church." It is his favorite way of describing the community of Christian believers. "Now ye are the Body of Christ," he says. The old body, nailed to the cross and stowed in the tomb, has been discarded. In its place Christ has taken on a new body, another organism through which to manifest himself to the world. "Christ has no hands but your hands, no feet but your feet." That is Paul's daring conception of the church; we, the company of Christians: his hands outstretched in service, his feet to run his errands of mercy, his voice to sound in the ears of men.

We come to the communion and are still welcome, even though we be morally imperfect. But if we come "not discerning the Lord's body," though we be pure as driven snow, we are not in the spirit of it. We

World Communion 115

remain aloof and isolated, uncommitted to one another and the whole company of Christ's people. This comes home to us with special force on World Communion Sunday. Today, across the wide world, from Geneva to Genoa, from Paris, Texas, to Paris, France, from Hawaii to the outer Hebrides, this is the "worthiness" that God demands of us: be joined in love.

"Let a man examine himself" and strike from his heart all that locks him within himself, his own land, his own sect. Let him stretch hands across the sea to grasp the hand of Solzhenitsyn, the Russian novelist, fighting his lonely battle on our behalf; let us stretch our hearts to include those two million Chinese Catholics, maintaining a witness with a shrinking band of ministers, since the last ordination took place in 1963. Let us go in spirit behind every curtain: iron, bamboo, and silken to affirm the name that is above every name.

"Examine yourselves" writes Paul in his second letter to the Corinthians, "to see whether you are in the Faith." Notice that definite article *the* faith. He is not asking them to whip up more faith. We all have plenty of faith, we exercise it every day. But is it faith in *the* faith? Certain graduates, as time goes on, get further away from their books, and the subject of which they were once masters, gradually and insensibly becoming sloppy and careless in their thinking, less responsible and disciplined in their scholarship. It is also perilously easy for us Christians gradually and unknowingly to drift into ways of thinking, judging, evaluating, and acting so that while still religious, we become less and less distinctively Christian.

We may still bear the Christian name, still use the Christian words and symbols, but almost without knowing it we may have substituted nationalism for Christianity; piety plus patriotism for the strong ethical demands of the Sermon of the Mount; our own liberal or conservative preferences for the word of the cross that sits in judgement on them both; our own feelings for the objective work of Christ. St. Paul says in another place, "I live by faith in the Son of God who loved me and gave himself for me"—but he did not, and would never have dreamed of saying, "I live by *my* faith in the Son of God."

Faith is not believing certain things about Christ because they are written in the Bible or handed down by tradition. It is having the courage to believe certain things about ourselves because they have been revealed to us in him and validated by him and because through Christ's faith we are drawn into a new relationship with God and with his world. So here in the presence of the bread and wine, we are recalled to what *the* faith is all about. Not our faith but God's Faith in us, manifested in our Lord Jesus Christ.

Youth Sunday

Jesus and Youth

> *One came up to him, saying, "Teacher, what good deed must I do to have eternal life?" Jesus said to him, "If you would be perfect, go, sell what you possess and give to the poor."*
>
> Matthew 19:16, 21

Today is Youth Sunday, and in preparation for it I've been looking into the wisdom of Jesus as it applies specifically to youth. I have to tell you quite frankly that there isn't much to go on! And what there is is rather disconcerting. The only time a young man is singled out for special mention in the New Testament, he is told by Jesus, "Go, sell what you have." And if young people then were like young people now, they didn't have much to sell! It isn't money and possessions that are youth's problem, but the lack of them!

But why this silence about young people in the teaching of Jesus? Why is it that we have no record of his advice to teen-agers? No specific sermons addressed to youth? Some of you here this morning have Jewish friends. So you know the words "Bar Mitzvah." That's the synagogue ceremony that marks the end of boyhood and the entry into manhood. It takes place, as you remember, at the age of thirteen. At thirteen in the Jewish community a boy officially becomes a man!

So you see, Jesus had nothing to say to teen-agers. There weren't any! The moment a boy entered his teens he became an adult.

That used to be true, years ago, in the Gentile world also. The school-leaving age in my father's day was thirteen, then in my day they raised it to fourteen. At fourteen, most of my companions and neighbors were out working in factories and mills and offices. I've just been reading the biography of the multimillionaire steel king, Andrew Carnegie, without whose great wealth we wouldn't have a public library system in America. Carnegie started work as a railway telegraph clerk at the age of fourteen. And even the kids who didn't go out to earn a living but proceeded to the university entered the university at what seems to us an astonishingly young age. John Milton matriculated at Cambridge before he reached his fourteenth birthday. The celebrated philosopher, John Stuart Mill, had his B.A. by the age of sixteen. But he was learning Greek and Latin at the age of five!

You see my point. If Jesus had nothing specific to say to teen-agers, it's because there weren't any teen-agers. What we call adolescence and think of as a fact of nature wasn't even invented. I say invented because Youth with a capital "Y" is just that—something made possible by machinery, by labor-saving devices, and by the affluent society. And like all inventions, it has created problems!

In the world to which Jesus spoke there were only two kinds of people, children and adults, and nothing in between. Sure, there were young adults and older

Youth Sunday

adults, but the same wisdom, the same teaching about life and duty was applicable to them all. So there's something a little odd about the New Testament even mentioning that this man was a young man. He must have been an interesting specimen, a rare bird. So let's look at him for a few minutes. Perhaps what marked him out from other adults was that he hadn't yet given up asking questions! Having heard that Jesus was a teacher of wisdom he came to him one day and asked, "Teacher, what must I do?" But as Christ's answer showed, what he was really asking was "How can I be perfect?" Which is a very young thing to ask, thank God! Senator Packwood of Oregon said lately on a "Meet the Press" program that most people who come to his office in Washington want something. The lobbyists come, wanting something that is good for them and their clients. It is only the young people, he says, who come asking "What is good for America?"

Well, there was this young man, centuries ago, asking not "What can you do for me?" but "What can I do?" But what a dusty answer he got! Jesus looked him in the eye and said, "If you would be perfect, go and sell all you have and give it to the poor." Now, if you young men and women took that command literally there wouldn't be much to go around, would there? Young people don't have much to sell in a material and physical sense. And if they shared everything they had with the poor, I doubt whether they would solve the poverty problem. Indeed, I don't doubt it at all: I know it would only make it worse!

Was Jesus wrong, then? No, he was not wrong.

Remember what he said was sell, not give away. To sell is to trade. When you sell something you don't just get rid of it. You enter the open market to get the best price you can. You act in a business-like manner to strike a bargain, to make a profit. Suppose then, we translate this sentence not, throw away all you have, but trade it in. And then you'll really have something to contribute to other people. Simply to make yourself poor is not going to make the poor richer!

As I read it, then, Christ's wisdom to the young is this: Sell! Be a salesman of your own possessions; make a profit on your own investment of youth, energy, brains, initiative. Many young people today want to give away what they don't have. In a world crying out for knowledge, for the technical application of knowledge to the enormous problems of modern life—ecological pollution, world-wide poverty, racial tensions—they take the apparently idealistic but lazy way of chanting slogans. They say they love everybody, black, white, and polka dot, but there's one thing more important than loving a Black or a Mexican-American, and that's getting him out of his ghetto, stimulating the economy, selling your skill to him. By developing your own talents, sharing your own education, you are giving something more important than material goods. I would go further and say that there's one more important thing than loving your fellow man, and that is making it possible for him to love you!

Paul Goodman, who wrote that very important book, *Growing Up Absurd,* had the most generous sympathy, the clearest insights I know into the problems of young people. He used to be the darling of the campuses. But later, he said, when he spoke with radical students he was met with sullen silence. "They want student power." But student power is the power to be a student, not an amateur politician. "I doubted," he said, "whether these people were authentically students at all." But isn't that their first responsibility? He asked them: "You want a new social order, but in any social order, whether it be Mao's or Castro's, would there not have to be engineers; wouldn't people get sick and need medical care?" "No!" they said, "It's important only to be human—the rest will follow!"

Now, let me give this a more personal twist. Whether we like it or not, we are all in the selling business. Shakespeare said in an anguished sonnet, "I have sold cheap what is most dear!" And from a very different source, Omar Khayyám, comes this rueful confession:

> Indeed the Idols I have loved so long
> Have done my credit in this World much wrong:
> Have drowned my Glory in a shallow Cup,
> And sold my Reputation for a Song.

In other words, the great tragedy of life is to sell yourself short; to exchange brain and brawn, youth and the electric energies of youth for swiftly fleeing, momentary sensations. When I was on the edge of leaving seminary, I consulted an elder statesman of the church. I have never forgotten the advice he gave me: "Sell yourself in the highest market!" He meant nothing as crass as "go for the biggest salary," but rather: "Go for the biggest job—go where you are needed most. Go where you will be fully used!"

Have you noticed how Jesus emphasized the profit motive? "What does it profit a man," he asked, "if he gain the whole world and lose his own soul?" To make a profit on your own life you just have to know how to choose. As Browning said, "Life's business being just the terrible choice." The difference between a life of increasing returns and a life of diminishing returns, between a self that is growing richer, more exciting every day and one that simply peters out is just this: choice, discrimination, selection. And selection above all in the ideas, the philosophy, the persons you decide shall master and command you. And if I point to Christ as the perfect master it is not because it is my duty to do so, but because he, and he supremely, masters men without crushing them, uses them in the most creative and rewarding fashion.

No truly great man has ever impoverished me. And the greater he is the more he releases me into being my true self. Little men, phony leaders, want to belittle me to make themselves great. But that truly great one, Jesus of Nazareth, has one desire, and one desire only; not my slavish imitation, but my genuine growth and development at the service of God's will.

The testimony of all the ages comes to focus in the Scottish prayer:

> Make me a captive, Lord,
> And then I shall be free;
> Force me to render up my sword,
> And I shall conqueror be. . . .

My will is not my own
Till Thou hast made it Thine;
If it would reach a monarch's throne
It must its crown resign:
It only stands unbent
Amid the clashing strife,
When on Thy bosom it has leant
And found in Thee its life.

Thanksgiving

Land of the Pilgrims' Pride

But as it is, they desire a better community, that is, a heavenly one. Therefore God is not ashamed to be called their God.
Hebrews 11:16

The first Thanksgiving dinner I ever sat down to was in Scotland. But it was not a Scottish dinner. There was no haggis! The Scots are as thankful as any other people, but they do not observe the fourth Thursday in November as a national holiday. So all the people present, except my wife and me, were Americans, and they were all students studying at Edinburgh University. We must have been the only people in the city taking time off—all the natives were working!

It comes as a little bit of a shock to Americans living abroad to discover that, unlike Christmas and New Year and Easter, which are universal, Thanksgiving is as American as apple pie. American students in foreign universities—and at any given moment there are thousands of Americans abroad—members of trade delegations; embassy staffs in Paris, London, Rome; newspaper men in Moscow or Madrid will be taking time out on Thursday to eat turkey and cranberry sauce and pumpkin pie, especially imported from home. And however well they fit into their environment on the other 364 days of the year, on Thursday they will stick out like a sore thumb, and be very, very self-consciously American.

For Thanksgiving is a peculiarly national festival. It celebrates that day in 1622 when Governor William Bradford summoned the survivors of the *Mayflower* to praise God for their first harvest—the first tangible sign that their pilgrimage had divine approval, that "God was not ashamed to be called their God."

Other nations give thanks, of course. One of the most popular services in an English church, often outcrowding Christmas and Easter, is Harvest Thanksgiving. The British really go in for that in a big way, decorating the sanctuary, not with a chaste bowl of flowers, but piling up on the altar the fruits of farm, field, and garden. And what a lovely smell—such a change from the usual odor of sanctity! And the singing! Suburban stockbrokers, who have ploughed up nothing but the golf course all year, expand their lungs to proclaim, "We plough the fields and scatter the good seed on the land/But it is fed and watered by God's almighty hand."

But only in America, to use Harry Golden's inspired phrase, is there a Thanksgiving, not only or not even chiefly as a sentiment of gratitude for the general goodness of God, but most emphatically for his particular goodness to this land and this people, for its origins, for that small company of men, women, and children, who landed at Plymouth Rock and laid the foundations of a new nation.

Whereupon we sing not only "Come Ye Thankful People Come" but also,

> Land where my fathers died,
> Land of the pilgrims' pride,
> From every mountainside
> Let freedom ring.

Of course, the word "pilgrim" has vastly extended its range since 1620. For wave after wave of pilgrims have surged onto these shores since then. I only wish that what Willa Cather did to make us aware of the Bohemian pilgrims, who made the epic journey across the sea and land to Nebraska, some brilliant novelist would do for the Germans who straggled ashore at Port Lavaca here in Texas—duped by empty promises, but still stubbornly determined to carve out a new life on this continent.

We are a nation of pilgrims. The word is as meaningful in New Braunfels as in New Hampshire, as meaningful in Minnesota as in Massachusetts. The English pilgrims were fleeing from English bishops, the Germans and Scandanavians from an oppressive state church, the Czechs, Poles, Russians were seeking liberty to breathe, act, think, and worship.

There are, as you know, two strains of immigrants that make up the American "melting pot." There were those who came to make a better life. Who shall blame them? Who wouldn't make every effort to leave a land where life was nasty, brutish, and short? But without being discriminatory, I think it is only right to say that the bigger and more creative contribution was made by those who straggled over here for reasons of faith, not fortune—the Puritans, the Huguenots, Menonites, Moravians, Waldensians, Amish, and Dunkers. These all, in the language of the New Testament, "showed plainly that they desired a better country"— not only a life without poverty, but a life without fear, a life wherein they could obey God and serve him according to conscience.

Of course, we all remember that the pilgrim consciousness disappeared from the national life for a long period of time. It was, in fact, 240 years after the first Pilgrim father sank to his knees at Plymouth that Thanksgiving day was reinstated on the calendar and proclaimed an official American holiday; and that was done at a time when things were going badly. Somebody once said that "all nations grow odious in prosperity." They certainly grow careless. And it took the tragedy of the Civil War and the scarred spirit of Abraham Lincoln to recall the pilgrim heritage, that such a recollection might bind up the nation's wounds. In Lincoln's words:

> We have forgotten the Gracious Hand which preserved us in peace, and multiplied and strengthened us, and vainly imagined all these blessings were produced by some superior virtue or wisdom of our own. Intoxicated by unbroken success we have become too self-sufficient to feel the necessity of redeeming and preserving grace; too proud to pray to the God who made us.

But, of course, the really important phrase in my text is the last, "wherefore God is not ashamed to be called their God." Isn't that a startling thing to say? What if God should become ashamed to be called our God? We are so humanistic in our theological thinking today, even those who label ourselves "religious," that such a possibility scarcely occurs to us. We actually imagine we are conferring upon God a favor by believing in him. But what if he should cease to believe in us? That was the haunting fear that smote the heart of Lincoln.

And that is why, with a stroke of genius, he sought to "bind up the nation's wounds" by seeking to instill into the divided national heart, its former unity, North and South, victors and victims, in their pilgrim beginnings. We all began as pilgrims, but we have become travellers—more anxious to cover the ground than, as our ancestors did, to colonize it.

We all tend to romanticize the past, but it is practically impossible to over-idealize our pilgrim ancestors. If I single out the New England men, the *Mayflower* men, the Puritans, it is only because I know their history better. But what was true of them is true of all proper pilgrims. They had tremendous courage in venturing here at all, leaving home and soil and kindred, and then, within a mere year or two of establishing a physical footing, establishing an intellectual, educational, and spiritual footing.

We talk about this as an age of speed! We flatter ourselves! Within ten years of landing at Plymouth Rock—back-breaking years of cultivating the soil and coping with the severe New England weather—those sturdy ancestors had established the town of Boston.

Five years later they began the famous Boston Public Latin School. A year later Harvard College was in existence. In 1640 the first American book was published. By 1647, twenty-seven years after landing on alien soil, there was a law passed requiring an elementary school in every town of fifty families. After a mere quarter of a century of Pilgrim government in Massachusetts that colony had an educational system that was not to be matched by the mother country for another two hundred years. That was the Pilgrim spirit. We should strive to maintain that spirit in our everyday lives.

Advent Sunday

Be Prepared

Prepare ye the way of the Lord, make his paths straight.

Matthew 3:3

It's a mystery to me why the word "prepare" should have such an ominous ring. Why does it sound more like a threat than a promise on the lips of most people, more like a grim warning than a joyous invitation? "Prepare to meet thy God!" Remember that text? Where did you see it last? Probably on the highway just as you got to a dangerous curve, chalked up by some religious bully who wanted to make your flesh creep. Or posted outside a fundamentalist tabernacle as though the good people inside were shaking their fists at you!

Why should preparation always be for disaster? For the day of judgement? For the rainy day? Actually, I find it easier to prepare for a rainy day than for a fine day. So did Noah, you remember. Noah was magnificently prepared for the flood, but he got drowned in a bottle! He was fully equipped to meet adversity: stinging winds and howling gales. What he was not ready for was prosperity. Battling the waves he could say,

> I am the master of my fate;
> I am the captain of my soul,

But when he got to dry land and those hills covered with grapes, he went down like a nine-pin. "And Noah was drunken," says the Bible bluntly.

And that's been the story of many a life. With what courage and dignity men have withstood the hammer blows of misfortune and poverty only to go to pieces at the touch of a feather. I could tell many a tale about that. One of the heroes of my boyhood was a deacon in the church I grew up in. He had climbed out of the gutter to become a pillar of the community. By sheer hard work, night school, dogged devotion to his job, he made good. And having reached the top he proceeded downhill slowly at first, then with gathering acceleration, unable to cope with wealth and power.

And what is true of individuals is often true of nations. We see it in the decline and fall of the Roman Empire. We may be seeing it in modern America. Perhaps it is an exaggeration to say with that crusty critic, John Jay Chapman, that "all nations are odious in prosperity," but history certainly shows that the better side of national life is more evidenced in its days of promise, of pioneering and struggle, than in its days of fat, sleek achievement.

"This was their finest hour!" said Churchill of his

beleagured countrymen hit night after night by Hitler's bombers. In some strange way, much to Hitler's chagrin, the British seemed to be prepared for peril and danger. By historical memory, with hidden reserves, it was better prepared for this than for the balmy days of peace.

"Prepare ye the way of the Lord!" If you think that applies only to Advent or to getting ready for Christmas or that it has only a religious application, then you haven't looked around you lately. In reality it announces a law that is applicable to the whole of life, and especially to the good things of life, to all that makes life lordly and rich and colorful and joyous. It's these things that have to be prepared for, with even greater care than life's storms and shadows.

Looking back over my own experience, it seems to me that I have missed out on all kinds of wonderful things, of significant and enriching experiences, because I just wasn't ready for them when they came. They came knocking at the door, and I wasn't there.

We talk about a man not being "all there" when he's mad. And there have been times when we were mad—mad at somebody, upset, preoccupied, filled with thoughts of resentment or vengeance, so jangled and upset that we couldn't enjoy what was offered to us. The fine day was overclouded, the sun shone, but not for us! You know what I mean. Unless there is serenity and peace without the preparation of putting our thoughts and feelings in order, the biggest things can happen and pass us by completely!

And what is true of inward experiences is true also

Advent Sunday 133

of outward success. The difference between one man and another isn't always a matter of capability or talent: it's sometimes just a question of readiness, of being prepared for the opportunity when it comes. If I may use the hackneyed illustration of Isaac Newton and the apple: apples were falling in profusion that autumn in 1662. In the orchards of England many men received a bump on the head, but only one man got the *idea* because his head was ready to receive it, because he had thought long and hard about the mystery of gravity. Or think of James Watt, waiting for his tea water to boil! A historian of science said that if the English were not a nation of tea drinkers there would have been no Industrial Revolution. But Tommy Watt and Mrs. Watt and Grandpa Watt were all tea drinkers; they had all idly noted the lid of the kettle dancing when the water boiled. It was only Jamie who got the message.

I was reading the other day about that prolific songwriter Frank Loesser. Somebody asked him how he thought up all those marvellous melodies. He couldn't explain it; the nearest he could come was, "Tunes simply pop into my head all day long." "But, of course," he added, "your head has to be arranged to receive them." Some people's heads are arranged so that they keep getting colds; his keeps getting songs.

Prepare to meet thy God! Whether thy god be music or inventions or inner happiness or moral achievement, the same rule holds. Why does one man have so many friends? It is because he's prepared to receive them. He has made himself capable of friendship.

Why does one man have such an exciting sense of the spiritual world and God present within it? It is because his life in all its parts is prepared through sensitive living and moral finesse to be a fit and efficient receiving apparatus.

This is why youth is so strategic a time. Sure, it's a great time in itself. But its importance lies in the kind of preparation it is making. Youth is squandered unless it is both good in itself and a readying for further good.

I forget who said it, but I shall never forget the words, for they have haunted me ever since I heard them. The two saddest sentences that can fall from a young man's lips are: "There's plenty of time yet" and "It's too late now!" Somewhere in between those two sentences lies, "Prepare ye the way of the Lord!" Do nothing that shuts you off from further growth, that bangs the door on an expanding future. There are such actions, there are such thoughts, there are such deeds; they block all future progress. And there are, thank God, ways of doing everything that makes possible an even finer next step.

There is theology in the Advent message, but I've chosen today to strip it to its most practical, personal terms. Divested of all jargon and abstractions, the Advent message is this: There are two ways of living life—open and shut.

You can read books that do nothing for you except kill time—a dreadful phrase! You can indulge in conversation that opens nothing up but is simply a rearrangement of what's been said a thousand times be-

Advent Sunday 135

fore. You can go about your business and even make a success of it and be dead inside. Or you can do all these things: read, talk, work, and make them all activities of growth and promise.

It was said of our great native philosopher, William James, by his sister Alice, that brother William seemed to be born afresh every morning. Yesterday had been a good day, but today was going to be even better. Yesterday he had two good ideas, today he was going to have three. He was always growing, always curious, always ready to push on from medicine, where he started, to philosophy to psychology, of which he was the American pioneer, to religion, on which he wrote the great classic "The Varieties of Religious Experience."

He prepared the way of the Lord. And he did it in a way that John the Baptist would have approved. He labored to make society and his country prepared for the spirit and ethos of Christ. For it is often forgotten that William James was not only an exciting, ever-expanding thinker, he was a doer. He projected and supported camps for unemployed men and aimless boys, where human energies could be turned to creative and dignified use. He not only coined the striking phrase, the "moral equivalent of war," he labored to prepare the minds of his countrymen to accept that as their destiny.

As you look around the world today, you see how accomplished we have all become about preparing for war, for disaster, for a possible attack on what we have and hold; but how miserably unprepared we are for peace, for fellowship, for the coming of the Lord—in his new power and glory.

Kierkegaard, the Danish thinker, called one of his great and difficult books *Stages on Life's Way*. There are, indeed, stages on life's way. Kierkegaard called them the Aesthetic, the Ethical, the Religious. A man begins by having an artistic distaste for bad form. He prefers good taste to vulgarity, beauty to ugliness, harmony to discord. But then he takes the further step: he feels the claim of moral demand upon him. He learns to use the word sin, an affront upon God's plan for his life. And when he takes morality seriously, he is on the frontiers of religion. He learns forgiveness and acceptance.

I wish we could all live so that life has stages on life's way!

Brutus has reminded us that

> There is a tide in the affairs of men,
> Which, taken at the flood, leads on to fortune;
> Omitted, all the voyage of their life
> Is bound in shallows and in miseries.

How foolish we should be to miss the tide!

Bible Sunday

Read, Mark, Learn, and Inwardly Digest

And he said to me, "Son of man, eat this scroll that I give you and fill your stomach with it." Then I ate it; and it was in my mouth as sweet as honey.

Ezekiel 3:3

The third Sunday in Advent is widely observed as Universal Bible Sunday. In the *Book of Common Prayer,* the collect for Bible Sunday begins, "Blessed Lord, who hast caused all holy Scriptures to be written for our learning," and continues with the vivid petition, "Grant that we may read, mark, learn, and inwardly digest them." Why! there's a whole theory of education behind those words!

Obviously, the literary style of the collect owes something to Francis Bacon ("Some books are to be tasted, others to be swallowed, and some few to be chewed and digested"), but the striking imagery is lifted bodily from the works of Ezekiel, poet, priest, and prophet. It was he who in his bold and earthy way first made the point that you don't get any nourishment out of the Bible unless you chew it, unless you take it into your system, unless, as he put it, you "eat" it.

This is true of all books, not only of the Bible. Some

years ago there was a famous bestseller called, *How to Read a Book*. I never got around to buying it because I was too busy reading books already! But I imagine what Mortimer Adler said was much what Ezekiel is saying here. To get the best out of a book, much more is involved than good eyesight or the ability to scan words on a page. This requires some measure of interest, a passion to know, the ability to get below the surface, to read between the lines, to sift the wheat from the chaff. A man's whole being has to be involved, not merely the top of his mind, but the bottom of his heart. Or, as Ezekiel puts it bluntly, his bowels—the whole personality.

If this is true of secular works, novels, biographies, poems, it is even more true of scripture—all scriptures, any scripture, from the Bible to the Koran, from the Upanishads to the Analects of Confucius. Every holy book is an interpretation of life, and you don't get anything out of an interpretation of life unless you are anxious to know what life means, unless you are looking for an interpretation that will give your own life significant direction.

Some time ago in the *Saturday Review* there was a cartoon which showed a plump matron flopped out on a divan, feet up, and a box of chocolates at her elbow. The caption read, "I love to curl up with a good book." And the book in her hand was entitled "Holy Bible!" But the Bible is not a "good book" in that sense. It is no volume for drooling away an empty evening. The Bible comes alive only when it is approached by people who are asking the ultimate questions, not speculative questions like "Who made the world?" or "Who made God?" but "Why was I made?" "To what end was I born, and for what cause came I into the world?" "What does it mean to be a man? In what direction am I moving?" This is what Ezekiel means by his picturesque expression about ingesting and digesting the scroll.

I remember how Ezekiel's words first came alive for me. One day outside the National Gallery, I happened to run into a friend I hadn't seen for years. You know how it is with some people: you don't have to see them often, but when you do, even after a number of years, you pick up the threads immediately. I noticed he was carrying a copy of Martin Buber's classic work, *I and Thou*. "Have you read it?" I asked. "Read it!" he said, "Why man, I eat it!" And I knew what he meant. He fell upon it like a famished man seeking food. He nourished himself on it. This man had been in such deep waters, his life shattered by so many personal tragedies, that when Buber's book appeared, he not only welcomed it intellectually, but he chewed over it, savored it, got it right down into his innards.

Some people (especially when it comes to the Bible) just swallow it hook, line, and sinker. It is the Bible, isn't it? Who are they to question it, argue with it, analyze and sift it? And the result is that great gobs of it stick in their throats. They read it, but they don't digest it, and it gives them the stomachache. They get spiritual dyspepsia. They're carrying the Bible instead of letting the Bible carry them! They're treating it as a fetish.

With Ezekiel's help let me try to spell out what it means to read the Bible. There is no more virtue in reading the Bible for its own sake than reading the telephone directory for its own sake. You consult the directory when, and because, you want to get in touch with someone. Of course, if you've got nothing better to do, you may leaf through it admiring the pretty names or marveling at the odd names or counting up the number of Smiths or chuckling over odd combinations.

And that isn't far off from how some people study the Bible! But the purpose of a directory, as I say, is to get in touch with someone, a doctor, a friend, a repairman. Some of these numbers are engraved on your heart, of course. A boy doesn't have to look up his sweetheart's number every time he calls her!

And there are certain things in the Bible a man doesn't have to look up either. I imagine most Christians don't need to read the Twenty-Third Psalm; they know it by heart, along with such other favorite passages as Paul's Hymn of Love, the Beatitudes, or bits of John, like "Let not your heart be troubled."

But the vision of reality we get from such passages is a very limited one. We should learn something about peace of mind and spiritual psychology, but there is more to life than that. The Lord of the Bible is not merely the Divine Healer; he is the Cosmic Disturber, the God who not only says "Come unto me and rest," but who says "Go, bear ye one another's burdens and so fulfill the Law of Christ."

The most profitable way of reading the Bible is not

to find out what God said many centuries ago to Abraham, Moses, Isaiah, or even Ezekiel. What God said to those gentlemen may be very interesting, but it might also be irrelevant. I'm not sure that everything God said to Moses is applicable to me. But I am quite sure that God was able to speak to Moses because Moses was the man he was. Because, if I may put it in a more sophisticated way—reality, experiences, events were meaningful to him, whereas for me, whole tracts of experience just don't say anything at all. I read the Bible not only to get the message given to other men but to discover why they got it, and under what conditions, and to find out the sort of person I need to become to hear his voice speaking to me. People sometimes say, "I've never heard God speak. I don't know what you mean by that!" And it never seems to occur to them that they might be deaf, that their receiving apparatus is so crude and jangled that nothing can get through on it.

The value of studying such men as Moses, Isaiah, and Abraham is to see the conditions under which the universe becomes a speaking universe, the conditions under which, as for the psalmist, "day unto day uttereth speech and night unto night showeth knowledge."

Why is it that these, and others like them, heard the voice of God? Not because they were psychic and not because they were mystics, but because like Abraham they went out not knowing whither they went, because like Moses they accepted leadership and responsibility for a nation yet unborn, because like

Isaiah they threw themselves into the fray for reformation, because like Paul on the Damascus Road they struggled with conscience until it became an agony.

Finally, why is Bible Sunday observed in Advent? What's the connection with Advent? Because the whole of the Bible, from cover to cover, from Genesis to Revelation, is concerned with the coming of God into human life. So the prayer rightly ends "that we may embrace and ever hold fast the blessed hope of everlasting life, which Thou hast given us in our Saviour Jesus Christ."

That is why it is such a tragedy that some so-called "Bible Churches" have usurped that name, but in the very act deny the spirit of the Bible. Their members, then, seem to me to be refugees from the modern world: people who want to keep religion pure. They want to be uninvolved with such worldly considerations as politics, economics, housing, and race relations. Their ambition is to keep politics out of religion and religion out of politics, which of course, is what the Russians want to do and what Hitler wanted in 1933.

A lot of so-called Bible study today may actually be a way of avoiding God, of safely embalming him in the past by becoming meticulously concerned with who Jesus was while conveniently ignoring what he said. As Dr. Joseph Fort Newton has said: "All my life I have heard the churches arguing about how Jesus came into the world and how he went out of it, while ignoring what he did, and taught us to do, in the world."

Bible Sunday

But it is not only the fundamentalists who misuse the Bible; devotees of the spiritual life and personal self-development turn to it for reasons that are foreign to its purpose. That fine Irish poet George Russell wrote:

> I have read all the sacred books which I could find, those of China, of Egypt, of India, of Persia, of Judaea, as well as the mystic philosophers like Plato, Plotinus and Sankara, and I have found truth in all, and a similiar identity of belief. I have found, however, that the sacred books of Judaea are the least interesting of all, and contain less spiritual truth than the Bhagavad-Gita or the Upanishads for example. The Old Testament is a collection of poems and legends far more than a collection of sacred texts which are profound.

Of course, he's right. If what you are looking for is golden sentences, helpful mottoes, inspirational poetry, or lovely thoughts—go elsewhere! That isn't what the Old Testament is about. It is about God's action in history, a history that is raw, crowded, muddled, and mistaken but redeemed by one salient fact: that through it all, within it all, guiding it all, shaping it all, is the purpose and action of God. It is not a "good book" like the *Meditations* of Marcus Aurelius. It is an open book. It is the story of God's dealing with a people, preparing them under the discipline of suffering, under the shaping hand of prophets and seers to receive Christ.

That is the meaning of the whole process: God's calling and election of Israel; God's care and education of Israel; God's refining and chastising of Israel; God's gracious dealing and forgiveness of Israel; all to this end—that Christ should come. All history, not only Hebrew, but American history; all scriptures, not only Judaea's but our scriptures, the Constitution, the Declaration of Independence, the Bill of Rights, remain unfulfilled until Christ opens them up for us, shows us that they point toward him and are fulfilled in him and his kingdom.

Christmas

God Bless You!

And the Word became flesh and dwelt among us, full of grace and truth; we have beheld his glory, glory as of the only Son from the Father.

John 1:14

When I was growing up in Wales, boys and girls used to go out caroling on Christmas Eve as boys and girls do all over the world. Some of the youngest of them didn't find it easy to remember the words. But there was one song they all sang with gusto because the words were easy to learn, much easier than "Hark, the Herald Angels Sing" or "The First Noel."

> Christmas is coming, the geese are getting fat,
> Please to put a penny in the old man's hat;
> If you haven't got a penny, a ha'penny, will do,
> If you haven't got a ha'penny, God bless you!

And that's what I want to say this morning: "God bless you!" Or in the words of the crippled Tiny Tim, "God bless us every one!"

But why should I say that? God has blessed us, hasn't he? Isn't that what Christmas means? By sending his Son into the world to lighten its darkness, to lift men's hearts, to fill their lives with love, he has already blessed us. That's why we're happy at Christmas. Not because we're expecting presents, although I'm sure the children hope they're going to arrive. But that's only part of it, because simply receiving gifts wouldn't make you happy, it might make you greedy!

What gives Christmas its glow, its warmth, and its joy is that somewhere tucked away, you have a gift that you are going to give to somebody you love. The joy of a Christmas present, whether you made it or bought it, is seeing the surprise, that happy smile on the face of the person you give it to.

And all because two thousand years ago the world got its first Christmas present from God—Jesus Christ. And ever since then, men, women, and children have known the joy of giving. And what a joy it is! For as Jesus said when he was a grown man and a great teacher: "It is more blessed to give than to receive." Or as Nietzsche said,

> Give, you can never give enough!
> Give all, all is not too much!

You know there are places in this wide world where people don't observe Christmas? I would hate to grow up in such a place, wouldn't you? It would take all the fun out of life. Sure, it would make life a lot easier. We wouldn't have to go shopping at the last minute, barging our way through crowded stores, puckering our brows, wondering whether that shirt will suit Dad's complexion or whether brother Bill would prefer golf balls or a nice frame for his girl friend's picture. They don't have problems like that in India, China, or Russia. But how much poorer they are without them! So when I say "God bless you!" I don't merely pray that he will bless. I congratulate you because he has already blessed you by putting into your hearts the desire to give and share and celebrate your life together.

Let me remind you of some other blessings that Christmas has already brought. One thing that the Christmas story makes very clear is that life is much more wonderful, much more mysterious and magical than appears on the surface. Remember how the story goes? When Jesus was born in Bethlehem in the days of King Herod, wise men came from the East to Jerusalem saying, "Where is he? For we have seen his star in the East and are come to worship him."

Did you ever hear such a mixture in all your life? "Bethlehem," a little village on a map, and it is still there. You can get there by plane, if you have the money for a ticket or don't get highjacked. Herod the king—you can read all about him in the history books, his date and deeds, the size of his palace, his cruelty, craft, and cunning. Jerusalem: another place. And the star! And angels singing! And lights flashing! And wise men worshiping! And shepherds rejoicing! What a mixture! What a glorious muddle of prose and poetry. Not at all neat and tidy like an engineer's plan, but more like a picture by Rembrandt, full of light and shade, gloom and glory, and the glory is more glorious because of the gloom, the light more splendid because of the shadows.

And that's life! There are hard facts, practical realities as we call them, but they are shot through with splendor and meaning. Sheep and singing, a cowshed like a cathedral, music and muck, romance and realism. Thank God it's not all brute fact and hard materialism. If Christianity has taught me anything, it is this: That people who try to live as though life were "nothing but"—nothing but food and shelter and sex, "nothing but" work or play, "nothing but" what appears on the surface—are not even getting the best out of these things.

What is food unless it is mixed in with friendship, laughter, and love? What is a house that is not a home? How can life be interpreted unless one takes account of what lies below the surface? That is why the Christmas story "blesses" me. It is so true to life. It wouldn't be the same story at all, it wouldn't be a "life" story if it were all angels and nicely antiseptic, deodorized, and "martinized," if the shepherds had joy in their hearts but no dung on their boots. The dung is as real as the delight, but this is where so many modern realists go wrong, the *delight* is as real as the dung!

Another "blessing" that comes to me at Christmas time is the blessing of wonder. Today we "know" so much, we can calculate so precisely, we can computerize the future so accurately, that we have lost the art of being surprised. Insurance men can tell us about how long we can expect to live; sociologists can tell us how many of us are probably going to end up in jail or in divorce court; educationalists can chart our learning capacity. On the IBM card there is no room for surprises, but there are plenty of them on the

Christmas card! There was a fifth-rate village and it brought forth a first-rate child. There was a little red school house in Nazareth that produced a genius, a man who has had more books written about him than any man who ever lived. There was a Jewish boy whose nationality half his followers didn't know, because he was always a citizen of the world. There was a man who attacked no religion, but has enriched them all. No world religion is the same as it was before he came, for they have all become self-conscious, weeding out their offensive elements: Hinduism its caste system, Buddhism its indifference to poverty.

> A Boy was born at Bethlehem that knew the haunts of Galilee,
> He wandered on Mount Lebanon, and learned to love each forest tree.
> But I was born in Marlborough, and love the homely faces there;
> I should not mind to die for them, my own dear *downs*, my comrades true;
> But that great heart at Bethlehem, He died for men He never knew.
> And yet, I think, at Golgotha, as Jesus' eyes were closed in death,
> They saw with love most passionate the village street at Nazareth.

That's the wonder of Christmas, and the Christ of Christmas. It is all so unexpected, it's all so unpredictable. In this open universe where God is our father, we aren't shut out by heredity or circumstances.

But to me the greatest blessing of Christmas is that

God's love is revealed. That's why we should never, however busy we are, spell Christmas, "Xmas." For "X" is an unknown quantity, and Christ took the "X" out of our lives when he came among us.

What Christmas says is that at the heart of the universe there is a person. "The power that moves the sun and the other stars" as Dante says. The force that fashioned the everlasting hills and the wayside flower, the energy that directs the march of history and the destiny of nations, is no passionless pulse of a machine, blind and uncaring, but more like the beating of a heart—the heart that beat in Christ.

And what men saw there once two thousand years ago is true eternally. "I stood at Naples once," said Browning, "a night so dark that nothing was visible. Then out of the clouds there came a lightning flash. It lasted but a second, but in that split second it lit up the whole landscape. One saw that within the darkness there was a city: ships, towers, theatres and temples, homes. The darkness closed in again and it all disappeared. But now I knew that it was all there." Christ was the lightning flash that revealed, in a moment of time, the eternal heart of God.

End of The Year

Live and Learn

I have learned, in whatever state I am, to be content. I know how to abound.
Philippians 4:11-12

"I have learned," says St. Paul. Let's ask ourselves, on this last Sunday of another year, what, if anything, we have learned. There's an old saying that "we live and learn." A friend of mine says ruefully, "We live anyway!" But what a tragedy if we do that and nothing more; if we are no wiser today, no closer to the heart of things, than we were at the beginning of the year.

I have learned, says the Scottish poet Edwin Muir, reaching middle age,

> I have learned when life's half done,
> You must give quality to the other half,
> Lest you lose both, lose all. . .

And then goes on to say, "Revise, omit, select, fill, fill deserted time."

"I have learned," says another fine poet, Cecil Day Lewis, in his "New Year's Eve" poem:

> To live the present, then, not to live for it . . .
> To court the commonplace. . . .

> Let me brood on the face of a field,
> The faces in streets, until each hero is honoured,
> Each unique blade revealed.
>
> ... And though my todays are
> Repetitive, dull, disjointed,
> I must continue to practise them over and over
> Like a five-finger exercise,
> Hoping my hands at last will suddenly flower with
> Passion, and harmonise.

"I have learned," says Martin Buber the philosopher, "that man cannot approach God by reaching beyond the human, only by becoming human."

"I have learned," said a great statesman, "that what is morally wrong can never be politically right."

And so I could go on for a long time citing the testimonies of distinguished persons. But let me try to share with you some of the wisdom that has become clearer to me this year. Most of it I should have known already, and perhaps did, but in a vague kind of way. But as Dr. Johnson once said, "The number of new things we need to know is small compared with the number of old things we need to be reminded of." Some of the things I have learned are negative in character: old copybook maxims that have sprung to new life, because they have been tested on my own pulse. Such well-worn wisdoms as "More haste, less speed." Or as Franz Kafka said, impatience is "one of the two cardinal sins from which all the others spring."

There are such negative discoveries, newly made,

End of the Year

as that "everything has to be paid for." The only difference is that we pay for some things right away and we pay for others in the long run, but the bill always comes in. And the question is, "Is it worth it?"

I have learned in the school of hard knocks, in the university of experience, that there are no shortcuts to anything worthwhile. The longer I live the more I realize that life is a journey and that we degrade it when we turn it into a trip. In fact, I have begun to hate and fear that word "trip." It has in it a suggestion of something cheap and nasty. People profess to take trips on chemicals, whereby (so they say) they "enlarge the consciousness."

I am old-fashioned (and I hope realistic) enough to believe that some things *do* enlarge consciousness. Science does since it enables human beings to range more freely through time and space. It reveals to us a variety of objects about which we would otherwise be ignorant. Literature enlarges consciousness. The library is still, despite Marshall McLuhan, vastly extending man's knowledge of his fellow man and making him more sensitive to him. Art is a great enlarger of consciousness. It helps us to appreciate the shapes and forms, the modes of life that lie around us. I still think these are the things that have lifted man out of the primitive chaos experience into which drugs and mystical "exercises" would land man back. The so-called trips upon which certain adventurous spirits embark are cheap substitutes for the real thing: a journey for which they are not prepared to pay the fare!

But let me turn now to some of the positive things I have learned, or relearned this past year. First and foremost is the supreme value of friendship. As Hilaire Belloc said, laughter and friendship are two things worth winning.

I liked the tone of it, but I didn't realize then that friendship is what life is all about. Nor did I realize how easy it is to lose the precious gift of friendship by sheer neglect, through simple laziness, by not making the effort to keep friendship in repair. It is a humiliating moment in a busy life when one realizes that one has many acquaintances, but few friends—not because one isn't friendly but because one has neglected to write an occasional letter and to make oneself available to share ideas.

Through Polonius Shakespeare said:

> Those friends thou hast, and their adoption tried,
> Grapple them to thy soul with hoops of steel.

A most unfortunate image, hoops of steel, for nothing kills friendship more than possessiveness! Friendship is nurtured not by grappling and holding in a steely grip, but by the silken cords of sensitivity, thoughtfulness, the relaxed desire to give and receive.

On the public stage, one thing I have learned, or relearned, is that what makes the headlines is not necessarily what makes news, and what makes news doesn't necessarily make history. Some of the most widely publicized movements of this year, the attention-grabbers will, I prophesy, be historical

End of the Year

curiosities in the near future. We will wonder what all the fuss was about. History is made by fine print, not by the banner headlines; not by those who shock us but by those who enlighten us. Religious history is not made by the expensively publicized rally, whose logical next step is another, bigger rally, if possible, but by the small group thinking together, working together to create morale, to inform and enlarge the mind, to essay face-to-face adventures in understanding and fellowship. There is still no substitue in religion for the family church and its quiet patient plodding routines of Sunday school teaching, pastoral care, regular worship.

One thing I am sure we have all learned is that the universe is a vastly bigger place than we used to think, but that the human eye is still the instrument that measures it. The human mind is still the instrument that uncovers its secrets. A clever man once said that "astronomically speaking, man is nothing," meaning that compared with the size of the universe man is a mere speck on the vast whirling fly wheel. To which a wiser man retorted that "astronomically speaking, man is the astronomer." It is his small but unique perception, his roving curiosity, his passion for truth that uncovered all those galaxies, not the other way about.

I have learned not to downgrade man but to upgrade him. He has a long way to go, but he has the capacity to go there if he wills. But that is the rub: if he wills. For, alas, the human heart is still the uncertain thing it always has been. We are capable of conquering outer space, but not inner space. Man, in spite of his triumphs, is still the man whom sin stains, sorrow wounds, death smites with its terrible tender sword. Worse still, he is agitated by triviality, upset by such primitive emotions as jealousy, distorted by anger, threatened by anxiety. We are terribly vulnerable people, and we live by two maps: the cosmic map that should lift us above our petty parochialisms, and a private map that can make a domestic tiff look like a world tragedy.

But the most important thing I have learned is the real nature of the religion I have professed for forty years. Like St. Paul I can say today, "I am not ashamed of the Gospel of Christ." Speaking in his own context Paul went on to say, "To the Jews it seems a stumbling block, to the Greeks foolishness." But this year with its alarms and excursions, its crises and tragedies, has revealed the utter bankruptcy of man's conventional wisdom.

A generation ago the golden rule was held up by some, and derided by others, as a shining but impossible ideal. Now it has become an absolute necessity if man is to salvage his civilization. A generation ago we were trying to adapt Christianity to modern conditions, today we are wondering how we can adapt modern conditions to Christianity before modern conditions swamp us all in chaos. Even an iconoclast like Bernard Shaw was moved to say at the end of his life, "I am ready to admit that after contemplating the world and human nature for nearly sixty years, I see no way out of the world's misery but the way Christ would have gone had He undertaken the work of a modern practical statesman."

One of the things I have learned and desire to learn even more fully in the coming year is the great difference between being dissatisfied and being unsatisfied. If I live until I'm one hundred, I shall always be unsatisfied, but I need not be dissatisfied. I shall always be uncontented but I need not be discontented.

We see lots of people around us today who are unhappier than they need be: jangled, querulous, frustrated because they haven't made this distinction. They have utopian, utterly unrealistic expectations of what life, marriage, parenthood, job, money, an all-electric kitchen will bring them. They will not come to terms with being unsatisfied as a perfectly natural state to be in, and so they become dissatisfied. "I have learned in whatever state I am," said that restless, ambitious, constantly moving man, "to be content." Paul was not satisfied, complacent, resigned, or passive. He was content. Behind that word content lies the Greek original *autarches* auto (self), arches (complete, fulfilled), in possession of inner resources.

But even in English the word "content" has two meanings. It may mean satisfied, but we also talk about the contents of a thing, meaning what it contains. And Paul was content-ful even when he was striving and unsatisfied. He had the full sense of living in the moment for eternal ends, because as he put it, his life was "hid with Christ in God."